# Editorial

The state of the family as an institution in our society is the subject of a great deal of current debate. *Social Focus on Families* brings together statistics from a wide variety of sources and uses charts, explanatory text and simple tables to paint a picture of UK families. It is aimed at a wide audience: policy-makers in the public and private sectors; market researchers; journalists and other commentators; the business community; academics, teachers and students; and the general public.

In looking at the family we have a broader canvas than for the previous titles in the *Social Focus* series which have covered children, women and ethnic minorities. We have been able to examine trends in family life, to look at dynamics, to investigate the real everyday changes that affect individual families, and to explore changing attitudes. *Social Focus on Families* gives a broad overview of a subject on which much in-depth research and analysis has already been done by others. Comprehensive further references are given for those who wish to explore the subject more deeply.

We would welcome readers' views on how the *Social Focus* series could be improved further and on topics which could be covered in future editions. Please write to us at the address shown below.

John Pullinger
Carol Summerfield
Office for National Statistics
1 Drummond Gate
LONDON SW1V 2QQ

# Contents

OFFICE FOR
NATIONAL
STATISTICS

Social

# Families

Editors:  John Pullinger
Carol Summerfield

Authors:  Peter Newman
Allan Smith

Production team:  Steve Whyman
Tony Symmonds
Phil Browne
Aspa Palamidas
Aysha Malik
Ted Snowdon
Alistair Price
Alyson Whitmarsh
Tim Harris

Graphics:  Michelle Franco

90 0368403 4

London: The Stationery Office

Also available in this series:

Social Focus on Children
£25      ISBN 0 11 620655 1

Social Focus on Women
£25      ISBN 0 11 620713 2

Social Focus on Ethnic Minorities
£25      ISBN 0 11 620793 0

**Symbols and conventions**

*Rounding of figures.* In tables where figures have been rounded to the nearest final digit, there may be an apparent discrepancy between the sum of the constituent items and the total as shown.

*Provisional and estimated data.* Some data for the latest year (and occasionally for earlier years) are provisional or estimated. To keep footnotes to a minimum, these have not been indicated; source departments will be able to advise if revised data are available.

*Non-calendar years.*
*Financial year* - eg 1 April 1995 to 31 March 1996 would be shown as 1995-96
*Data covering more than one year* - eg 1992-93, 1993-94 and 1994-95 would be shown as 1992-1995

*Units.* The main unit used in each table is shown at the top of the table. Where a table also contains data in a different unit this is labelled against the relevant row or column. Figures are shown in italics when they represent percentages.

*Symbols.* The following symbols have been used throughout *Social Focus*:
|  |  |
|---|---|
| .. | *not available* |
| . | *not applicable* |
| - | *negligible (less than half the final digit shown)* |
| 0 | *nil* |

Page

# Family living standards 29

2

# Contents

# Introduction

Most of us live in families, but fewer than half of us now live in a 'traditional' family containing a married couple with children. In recent years change has been rapid and the composition of families has become much more diverse. We have a greater chance of experiencing family change and different types of family structure.

*Social Focus on Families* brings together data from many different sources to paint a picture of families' lives in Britain today and how they have changed over the years. In general, the term family in the report refers to the 'nuclear' family, which excludes relations other than parents and their children. There were 15.8 million of these families in Great Britain in 1994. The 'extended' family which includes other relations is also of interest and contact with these relatives is also discussed in the report.

Over the last generation the traditional stereotype family has been on the decline as cohabiting couples and lone parents have become much more common. In addition, the number of multi-family households has fallen and there has been a dramatic rise in people living by themselves. Despite this, the majority of people still live as part of a family.

The type of family in which people live often changes at different stages of their lives. Families are in a continual process of change. Major changes in patterns of marriage, divorce and parenthood have had significant effects on the composition of families. In one generation the numbers marrying have halved and the numbers divorcing have trebled while the proportion of children born outside marriage has quadrupled. In addition, more people now cohabit either before, or instead of, marriage.

Most women have children at some point in their lives but there have also been some notable changes in family building trends. The average age at marriage has increased, family sizes have fallen and there has been a distinct trend towards women having children later in life. The reasons for this delay are thought to include the greater participation of women in higher education, the increasing proportion of women who continue working and want to develop their career before starting a family and women's improved control over their fertility through contraception.

Most children live with both parents, whether they are married or cohabiting, but there has been a substantial growth in lone parent families over the last 25 years. Lone parents now head almost a quarter of all families with dependent children, three times the proportion in 1971. There are many more lone mothers than lone fathers and this generally reflects the tendency of children to remain with their mother when a partnership breaks up.

The economic characteristics of families have also changed dramatically over the last few decades. The increasing proportion of women entering the labour market, continuing to work after marriage and returning to employment after childbirth means that the traditional model of 'breadwinner husband and homemaker wife' has been eroded. The most significant change in the working patterns of families has been the fall in the number of families living solely on a man's wages, and the related increase in the number of dual earner families. Attitudes have also changed with fewer people thinking that a wife's job is to look after the home and family than did so ten years ago.

# Introduction

Children have a significant impact on the working arrangements of parents. Women are usually most affected, particularly when their children are of pre-school age. However, they are now much more likely to return to work after childbirth than in the past. When mothers do return to work, their childcare needs are mostly met by members of their extended family. Even so, there is evidence that the traditional gender roles still exist in the home with women bearing the greater responsibility for looking after children and doing routine household chores.

There are also notable differences in the living standards of different types of families. Lone parent families tend to have lower incomes, and be more dependent on benefits, than other families. Consequently, they spend less than other types of families, and a greater proportion of their expenditure goes on food and other essentials such as fuel, light and power. They are also more likely to rent their housing and live in overcrowded and poorer quality accommodation than other families.

Despite the changing economic and social characteristics of families in recent years, the family continues to be an important institution in society. Families provide an invaluable source of informal care and support for individuals, particularly the elderly. Indeed, extended family members tend not to be scattered far and wide. Most maintain regular contact with their close relatives and the majority take part in a family gathering at Christmas. All in all, families continue to play a very central role in people's lives.

Social Focus on Families, © Crown copyright 1997

# 1

# Family dynamics

## Family structure and change

The traditional idea of a family is that of a married couple with children living with them. However, the prevalence of this type of family in society has declined as a result of changes in cohabitation, marriage, divorce and parenthood as well as the ageing of the population. Family structures have now become much more diverse. The recent patterns in family dynamics also mean that individuals are much more likely to experience a greater variety of family structures during their lifetimes. Wider family networks are also of interest and Chapter Three examines family relationships.

In general a standard definition of the family, often referred to as the nuclear family, has been used throughout this report (see box on page 11). However, in some cases other definitions have had to be used, such as that based on benefit units which has been used in the Income section of Chapter Two.

It is important to distinguish between the terms 'household' and 'family'. A household can contain one or more families and also household members other than those belonging to a nuclear family, such as members of the extended family, friends,

# 1.1

## Families and households

**Great Britain**

Millions

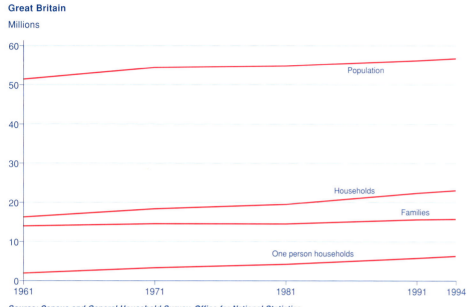

Source: Census and General Household Survey, Office for National Statistics

# 1.2

## People in households: by gender and family type, Spring 1996

**United Kingdom**      Percentages

|  | Males | Females | All |
| --- | --- | --- | --- |
| **Couples** | | | |
| Dependent children | 43 | 38 | 40 |
| Non-dependent children only | 11 | 8 | 10 |
| No children | 24 | 22 | 23 |
| **Lone parents** | | | |
| Dependent children | 6 | 11 | 9 |
| Non-dependent children only | 3 | 3 | 3 |
| **People not living as part of a family** | 14 | 17 | 16 |
| **All people in households** (=100%)(millions) | 28.5 | 29.4 | 57.9 |

Source: Labour Force Survey, Office for National Statistics

lodgers, visitors, flatmates or long-term guests. The most common type of non-family household is a person living alone, that is, a one person household. However, data on households can provide a valuable insight into the structure of families.

The 1961 Census was the first to satisfactorily distinguish families from households. The total number of families in Great Britain has grown over the last 30 or so years to 15.8 million in 1994 (Chart 1.1) while the number of households has increased at a much faster rate. This is mostly the result of the growth in one person households, as more adults are living alone. In addition, the increase in the number of people over pensionable age has changed the profile of the population. However, it is also partly because multi-family households have become less common.

In 1994 there were 23.1 million households in Great Britain and virtually all of these were either one family or one person households. Multi-family households accounted for less than 1 per cent of all households in 1994 compared with 3 per cent in 1961. In the 1970s and 1980s there was emphasis on the provision of first public, and then private, housing which encouraged families and single adults to live in their own separate accommodation. In particular, lone parent families, who historically were more likely than other families to live in multi-family households, have increasingly been living on their own.

In Spring 1996, 84 per cent of the population living in private households in the United Kingdom lived in a family headed by either a couple or lone parent (Table 1.2). More

# 1.3

people lived in the so-called 'traditional' family than in any other type of family; 40 per cent of people lived in a family comprising a couple with dependent children.

In 1995-96 almost four out of five of all families in the United Kingdom were headed by a married couple, either with or without children. Of the other families, more were headed by a lone parent than by a cohabiting couple.

These totals do, however, mask the effect that the age of the head of the family has on family type. More than nine in ten families where the head was aged 60 and over were married couples and most of these did not have any children living with them. In contrast, among families where the head was aged under 60, more than a quarter were cohabiting couples or lone parents in 1995-96 (Table 1.3). Dependent children were also present in the majority of families where the head was aged under 60. However, the proportion of families comprising a married couple with dependent children has declined during the 1990s continuing the trend of the last 30 or so years.

The social class of families also varies between different family types. Data from the 1991 Census can be used to identify patterns in the social class profiles of both men and women aged 20 to 49 based on their occupations, according to the type of family in which they live. A greater proportion of both men and women in married couples with dependent children were in the non-manual classes than those who were cohabiting with dependent

children. In addition, the social class profiles of lone parents with dependent children were more weighted towards the manual classes than their counterparts in married couples.

There are geographical variations in the prevalence of different types of families across Great Britain. In 1991 the areas where the proportions of all families who were married couples with dependent children tended to be highest were rural or semi-rural while inner city districts had the lowest proportions. In contrast, for cohabiting families with dependent children and lone parent families with dependent children, the reverse was generally true. For example, the proportion of families with dependent children who were headed by a cohabiting couple ranged from almost 14 per cent in the London Borough of Southwark to just under 2 per cent in the Western Isles of Scotland. Married couple families without children were most common, relatively, in areas of retirement or of population growth caused by migration, such as the South West, East Anglia, Wales and the South Coast.

## Families[1]: by type, 1990-91 and 1995-96

| United Kingdom | | Percentages |
|---|---|---|
| | 1990-91 | 1995-96 |
| **Married couples** | | |
| Dependent children | 44 | 41 |
| Non-dependent children only | 11 | 9 |
| No children | 22 | 23 |
| All married couples | 77 | 73 |
| **Cohabiting couples** | | |
| Dependent children | 3 | 4 |
| Non-dependent children only | - | - |
| No children | 5 | 7 |
| All cohabiting couples | 8 | 11 |
| **Lone parents** | | |
| Dependent children | 12 | 13 |
| Non-dependent children only | 4 | 3 |
| All lone parents | 15 | 16 |
| **All families** | 100 | 100 |

1 Head of family aged 16 to 59.

*Source: General Household Survey, Office for National Statistics; Continuous Household Survey, Northern Ireland Statistics and Research Agency*

**Family:** either a married or cohabiting couple, with or without their never-married children, who have no children of their own, or a lone parent with such children. This definition is essentially that of a nuclear family as it excludes relations other than parents and children. Step-children and adopted children belong to the same family as their step-parents or family that adopted them. Foster children, however, are not part of their foster parents' family as they are not related to their foster parents.

**Dependent children:** people aged under 16, or single people aged between 16 and 18 and in full-time education.

# 1.4

## Families with dependent children: by ethnic group, Spring 1996

**Great Britain** — Percentages

| | White | Black | Indian | Pakistani/ Bangladeshi | Other groups[1] | All ethnic groups[2] |
|---|---|---|---|---|---|---|
| Couples | 78 | 44 | 87 | 83 | 72 | 77 |
| Lone parents | 22 | 56 | 13 | 17 | 28 | 23 |
| | | | | | | |
| All | 100 | 100 | 100 | 100 | 100 | 100 |

1 Includes those of mixed origin.
2 Includes those who did not state their ethnic group.
**Source: Labour Force Survey, Office for National Statistics**

# 1.5

## Adults[1] in households: by gender, age and family type, Spring 1996

**United Kingdom** — Percentages

| | Couples | | | Lone parents | | All in families |
|---|---|---|---|---|---|---|
| | Dependent children | Non-dependent children only | No children | Dependent children | Non-dependent children only | |
| **Males** | | | | | | |
| 16-24 | 37 | 27 | 7 | 8 | 7 | 85 |
| 25-34 | 41 | 10 | 22 | 1 | 5 | 79 |
| 35-44 | 64 | 5 | 12 | 2 | 3 | 86 |
| 45-54 | 36 | 22 | 27 | 1 | 3 | 88 |
| 55-64 | 7 | 18 | 57 | .. | 2 | 84 |
| 65-74 | 1 | 8 | 68 | .. | 2 | 79 |
| 75 and over | .. | 4 | 59 | .. | 3 | 66 |
| | | | | | | |
| All aged 16 and over | 33 | 14 | 30 | 2 | 4 | 83 |
| **Females** | | | | | | |
| 16-24 | 37 | 18 | 11 | 14 | 5 | 86 |
| 25-34 | 47 | 4 | 20 | 15 | 2 | 88 |
| 35-44 | 61 | 6 | 11 | 13 | 2 | 93 |
| 45-54 | 23 | 23 | 32 | 4 | 5 | 89 |
| 55-64 | 2 | 13 | 58 | 1 | 5 | 79 |
| 65-74 | .. | 5 | 50 | .. | 4 | 60 |
| 75 and over | .. | 1 | 25 | .. | 5 | 32 |
| | | | | | | |
| All aged 16 and over | 28 | 10 | 28 | 8 | 4 | 78 |

1 Percentage of adults in each age group who lived in each family type.
**Source: Labour Force Survey, Office for National Statistics**

Distinctive patterns of family composition between the various ethnic groups in Great Britain provide yet further variety. Among families with dependent children, almost four out of five of those from the White group are couple families (Table 1.4). Among South Asians, that is those of Indian, Pakistani or Bangladeshi origin, an even greater proportion are couple families.

South Asian families also tend to be larger and are more likely than those from other ethnic groups to live in households of two or more families. Thus South Asian households may contain three generations with grandparents living with a married couple and their children. In contrast, just over a half of families with dependent children from the Black group are lone parent families.

It is important to realise that families are not static structures but are in a continual process of change. As young adults we either remain with our parent(s) as part of a family, or move away to either form another family if we cohabit, marry or have children, or to live independently. Around 85 per cent of young people aged 16 to 24 in the United Kingdom were living in a family in Spring 1996 (Table 1.5) and the large majority of these were living as part of a couple family.

People in their twenties and thirties are even more likely than young people to live in couple families as a greater proportion start to cohabit or marry during these years of their lives; the majority of adults in these couples have dependent children. Adults in older age groups are increasingly likely to be part of a couple with no children because either they have formed new partnerships without children or their children have left home. Late in life adults, particularly women, are more likely to live alone, usually because their partner has died. Nearly 70 per cent of women aged 75 and over were not living as part of a family in Spring 1996 which was double the proportion for men of the same age. This reflects the tendency for women to marry men older than themselves and have a greater life expectancy than men.

The composition of families can change over time because of any one of a number of factors. Family structures can be affected by natural changes such as a couple having a child, or other changes such as a couple separating. Results from the British Household Panel Survey (BHPS) show that families with children were much more likely than those without children to have experienced family change between 1994 and 1995 (Table 1.6).

For both couples with non-dependent children only and lone parents with non-dependent children only, by far the most common cause of change was the departure of children. The most likely change for couples with dependent children was the birth of a child, while for lone parents with dependent children it was joining a new partner. Couples with no children were the least likely to be affected by family changes which is probably not surprising as these families have a higher age structure than other family types.

There is evidence to suggest that the likelihood of people experiencing some family events such as cohabitation, marriage, the birth of a child or marriage breakdown in their early adult life has changed considerably over the years. Chart 1.7 looks at the proportion of women in Great Britain who had experienced a family event before the age of 25. For women aged 25 to 29 at the time of interview, about two fifths had given birth before the age of 25

compared with almost three fifths of women aged 50 to 54. Similarly, just under a half of women aged 25 to 29 were married before the age of 25 compared with about four fifths of those aged 50 to 54.

**Adults'[1] experiences of family change, 1994 to 1995**

**Great Britain**                                                                   Percentages

|  | Couples | | | Lone parents | |
|---|---|---|---|---|---|
|  | Dependent children | Non-dependent children only | No children | Dependent children | Non-dependent children only |
| **No change** | 86 | 76 | 93 | 82 | 83 |
| **Changes** |  |  |  |  |  |
| Birth of child | 6 | 0 | 3 | 2 | . |
| Departure of child | 5 | 22 | . | 8 | 14 |
| Separation from partner | 3 | 1 | 2 | . | . |
| Death of partner | 0 | 1 | 1 | . | . |
| Join new partner | . | . | . | 9 | 1 |
| Other changes | 0 | 0 | 1 | 0 | 2 |
| All changes | 14 | 24 | 7 | 18 | 17 |
| **All adults[1]** | 100 | 100 | 100 | 100 | 100 |

1 Aged 16 and over.
*Source: British Household Panel Survey, ESRC Research Centre on Micro-social Change*

# 1.7

**Experience of family events by women before age 25: by age[1], 1992-1995[2]**

**Great Britain**

Percentages

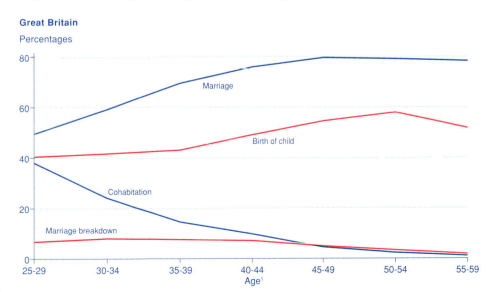

1 Age at time of interview.
2 Combined years: 1992-93, 1993-94 and 1994-95.
*Source: General Household Survey, Office for National Statistics*

# 1.8

## Attitudes[1] towards marriage and parenthood, 1994

Great Britain
Percentages

|  | Strongly agree/ agree | Neither agree nor disagree | Disagree/ strongly disagree | Can't choose/not answered | All |
|---|---|---|---|---|---|
| It is alright for a couple to live together without intending to get married | 64 | 15 | 19 | 2 | 100 |
| It is a good idea for a couple who intend to get married to live together first | 58 | 22 | 18 | 2 | 100 |
| People who want to have children ought to get married | 57 | 14 | 27 | 2 | 100 |
| Divorce is usually the best solution when a couple can't seem to work out their marriage problems | 53 | 23 | 20 | 4 | 100 |
| One parent can bring up a child as well as two parents together | 35 | 17 | 46 | 2 | 100 |
| The main purpose of marriage these days is to have children | 17 | 18 | 62 | 3 | 100 |
| It is better to have a bad marriage than no marriage at all | 2 | 4 | 92 | 2 | 100 |

1 People aged 18 and over were asked how much they agreed or disagreed with each statement, on a 5-point scale ranging from 'strongly agree' to 'strongly disagree'.

**Source: British Social Attitudes Survey, Social & Community Planning Research**

Many women are choosing to cohabit either before, or instead of, marriage. Over the last three decades there has been a dramatic increase in the proportion of women who have cohabited with a partner before their twenty fifth birthday. Almost 40 per cent of women who were aged 25 to 29 at the time they were interviewed had cohabited before the age of 25 whereas the proportion was just over 2 per cent for those aged 50 to 54.

This increase in cohabitation does not fully account for the decline in marriage; a lower proportion of women aged 25 to 29 had formed any union, that is had either married or had cohabited, before the age of 25 than was the case for older women. In addition, the trend in women's experience of marital breakdown before their twenty fifth birthday has shown a large increase; almost twice as many 25 to 29 year old women as those aged 50 to 54 reported that they had experienced this before the age of 25.

In the 1994 British Social Attitudes Survey (BSA), carried out by Social & Community Planning Research, respondents were asked to what extent they agreed, or disagreed, with a series of statements about different family structures and circumstances. Nearly two thirds of people agreed with the statement that 'it is alright for a couple to live together without intending to get married' while a slightly lower proportion agreed that 'it is a good idea for a couple who intend to get married to live together first' (Table 1.8).

Just 2 per cent of respondents thought that 'it is better to have a bad marriage than no marriage at all' and only one in five disagreed with the statement that 'divorce is usually the best solution when a couple can't seem to work out their marriage problems'. People who believed that 'one parent can bring up a child as well as two parents together' were outnumbered by those who disagreed.

The BHPS also asked people in 1994 if they thought that 'living together outside of marriage was always wrong'. People in the older age groups were more likely than those in younger groups to think that cohabitation was always wrong. Forty per cent of men who were aged 64 or over agreed with the statement compared with just 7 per cent of 16 to 34 year old men - perhaps a reflection of changing attitudes.

# 1.9

## Cohabitation, marriage and divorce

The trends in cohabitation, marriage, divorce and parenthood are some of the major factors that determine family structure and cause family change. These family dynamics are linked and particularly affect those in early to mid adult life. This is the period that usually covers the most significant family changes in a person's lifecycle such as leaving the parental home, forming a partnership, long-term union or getting married, having children and, for some, separation, divorce and lone parenthood.

One of the major changes in family patterns in recent decades has been the dramatic increase in the proportion of couples who have cohabited with their future marriage partner before marrying. Only a very small proportion of females, 4 per cent, whose first marriage was in 1966 had lived with their future husband before marriage (Chart 1.9). This increased rapidly to 68 per cent for those who were first married in 1993. The corresponding percentages were higher for women who were marrying for the second time, increasing from 24 per cent to 86 per cent. Results from the BHPS have also suggested that before cohabiting with their future spouse, people have increasingly lived with other partners in earlier relationships.

In 1995-96 one in ten 18 to 49 year old women in Great Britain were cohabiting compared with fewer than one in thirty in 1979. In recent years however, the General Household Survey (GHS) and Continuous Household Survey have asked questions on cohabitation to a broader age range of people in the United Kingdom. People in their twenties are the most likely to cohabit, although women tend to cohabit at younger ages than men (Table 1.10). The peak age group for women is 20 to 24, with one in five women cohabiting, while for men it is the 25 to 29 age group, with a slightly higher proportion cohabiting. Among the non-married population only, just over a fifth of people in Great Britain were cohabiting in 1995-96. Furthermore, about three in ten non-married 25 to 34 year olds were cohabiting.

In addition to the general increase in the proportion of people cohabiting there has also been a shift towards people cohabiting for longer periods. Both of these factors have undoubtedly contributed to the increase in people's age when they first marry.

### Pre-marital cohabitation of women: by year of marriage, 1989-1994[1]

**Great Britain**

Percentages

1 Data for first marriages relate to the combined years 1990-91 to 1993-94. Data for second marriages relate to the combined years 1989-90 to 1993-94.

*Source: General Household Survey, Office for National Statistics*

# 1.10

### Percentage of adults cohabiting: by age and gender, 1995-96

| United Kingdom | | Percentages |
|---|---|---|
| | Males | Females |
| 16-19 | 1 | 4 |
| 20-24 | 13 | 20 |
| 25-29 | 22 | 17 |
| 30-34 | 13 | 10 |
| 35-39 | 9 | 8 |
| 40-44 | 5 | 5 |
| 45-49 | 6 | 4 |
| 50-54 | 4 | 3 |
| 55-59 | 2 | 3 |
| All aged 16 to 59 | 9 | 8 |

*Source: General Household Survey, Office for National Statistics; Continuous Household Survey, Northern Ireland Statistics and Research Agency*

# Cohabitation, marriage and divorce

## 1.11

### Marriages and divorces

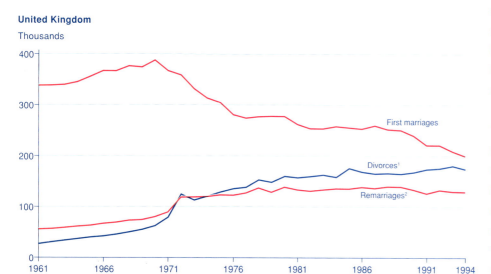

**United Kingdom**

Thousands

1 Including annulments.
2 For one or both partners.

*Source: Office for National Statistics; General Register Office for Scotland; Northern Ireland Statistics and Research Agency*

## 1.12

### Marriages, 1971 and 1994

| United Kingdom | Percentages | |
| --- | --- | --- |
| | 1971 | 1994 |
| **First marriage for both partners** | *80* | *61* |
| **First marriage for one partner only** | | |
| Bachelor/divorced woman | *5* | *10* |
| Bachelor/widow | *1* | *1* |
| Spinster/divorced man | *5* | *10* |
| Spinster/widower | *1* | *-* |
| **Second (or subsequent) marriage for both partners** | | |
| Both divorced | *4* | *14* |
| Both widowed | *2* | *1* |
| Divorced man/widow | *1* | *1* |
| Divorced woman/widower | *1* | *1* |
| **All marriages** (=100%) | | |
| (thousands) | *459* | *331* |

*Source: Office for National Statistics; General Register Office for Scotland; Northern Ireland Statistics and Research Agency*

Among never married women in Great Britain, not only did the number who were cohabiting rise rapidly but the average length of cohabitation increased, from 18 months in 1979 to 28 months in 1993-94. Among divorced people the period of cohabitation also increased considerably - from 36 months for men and 38 months for women in 1987 to 45 and 49 months respectively in 1990-91 to 1993-94.

Divorced people tend to cohabit for the longest time. Among those who were cohabiting in the early 1990s, seven out of eight divorced people had been cohabiting for more than a year compared with just over three quarters of single people and about two thirds of separated people. Indeed, more than half of those cohabiters who were divorced had been living with their partners for at least three years. Separated people were most likely to have been cohabiting for the shortest time because in most of these cases the marriage had come to an end

more recently than for divorced people. It should be noted that separated people, strictly speaking, are still legally married; however, because they can cohabit they have been included in the non-married category.

The increase in the incidence, and the trend towards longer durations, of cohabiting has, not surprisingly, coincided with a decline in the number of people marrying. The number of first marriages in the United Kingdom has decreased substantially since 1970 (Chart 1.11). In 1994 there were 201 thousand first marriages, which was a fall of 48 per cent from the peak number in 1970. Trends in the number of divorces are discussed in the text around Table 1.16.

In total there were 331 thousand marriages in the United Kingdom in 1994 and just over three in five were first marriages for both partners (Table 1.12). Remarriages have increased rapidly, almost doubling between 1971 and 1994 as a proportion of all marriages. The most common type of remarriage in 1994 was where both partners were remarrying after divorce, and divorcees were much more likely to remarry than widows or widowers at any age.

The decline in the number of first marriages is linked to the increase in the average age of men and women when they first marry. Between 1971 and 1993 the average age in Great Britain when marrying for the first time rose from 25 years to 28 years for men and from 23 years to 26 years for women. Again, the growing popularity of pre-marital cohabitation goes some way to explaining this trend, but other factors such as the increased and longer participation of people, particularly women, in further and higher education have also contributed.

Women tend to marry at younger ages than men. Around 5 per cent of women who first married in 1994 in the United Kingdom were teenagers compared with just under 2 per cent of men (Table 1.13). Conversely, only 16 per cent of women who married for the first time in 1994 were 30 or over compared with about a quarter of men. Just over a fifth of first marriages involved brides and grooms who were both in the 25 to 29 age group and in a further fifth of first marriages both partners were aged between 20 and 24.

Chart 1.14 shows marriage patterns for people in England and Wales. The trend among those born in the first half of the century was of decreasing age at marriage and, among women, increasing likelihood of marrying. About 90 per cent of women born in 1925 were married by the time they were 40, whereas 95 per cent of women born in 1945 were married by this age. The line shown on the chart for those born in 1965 is incomplete, as these people were only in their late twenties in 1994. However, a smaller proportion of women born in 1965 were married at most ages than those born in 1925 and 1945 - a clear indication that trends have changed. Similarly, for men, the proportion who were married by the time they were in their late twenties was lower for those born in 1965 than those born in 1945 and 1925.

As well as smaller proportions of people getting married, over the past few decades the trend has also been for first marriages to last for successively shorter periods of time, particularly for those in the younger age groups. For both men and women in Great Britain, 4 per cent of first marriages starting between 1965 and 1969 ended within three years; twenty years later these proportions had more or less doubled.

### Age combinations at first marriage, 1994

**United Kingdom** — Percentages

| | Age of husband | | | | | | |
| --- | --- | --- | --- | --- | --- | --- | --- |
| | Under 20 | 20-24 | 25-29 | 30-34 | 35-39 | 40 and over | All ages |
| **Age of wife** | | | | | | | |
| Under 20 | 0.8 | 3.1 | 1.1 | 0.2 | - | - | 5.3 |
| 20-24 | 0.7 | 18.8 | 17.1 | 3.4 | 0.5 | 0.1 | 40.5 |
| 25-29 | 0.2 | 6.1 | 21.8 | 8.4 | 1.5 | 0.3 | 38.3 |
| 30-34 | - | 0.9 | 4.0 | 5.1 | 1.6 | 0.5 | 12.1 |
| 35-39 | - | 0.1 | 0.5 | 0.8 | 0.8 | 0.4 | 2.7 |
| 40 and over | - | - | 0.1 | 0.2 | 0.2 | 0.6 | 1.1 |
| All ages | 1.8 | 29.0 | 44.5 | 18.1 | 4.6 | 1.9 | 100.0 |

*Source: Office for National Statistics; General Register Office for Scotland; Northern Ireland Statistics and Research Agency*

# 1.14

### Men and women married by certain ages: by year of birth

**England & Wales**

Percentages

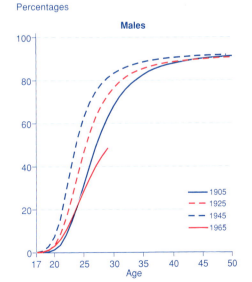
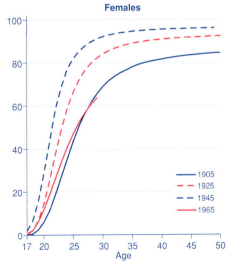

*Source: Office for National Statistics*

# 1.15

## Women separated within five years of first marriage: by year of, and age at, marriage, 1995-96

| Great Britain | | Percentages | |
| --- | --- | --- | --- |
| | Age at marriage | | |
| | Under 20 | 20-24 | 25-29 |
| **Year of marriage** | | | |
| 1965-1969 | 10 | 7 | 2 |
| 1970-1974 | 15 | 5 | 3 |
| 1975-1979 | 17 | 9 | 12 |
| 1980-1984 | 14 | 11 | 5 |
| 1985-1989 | 33 | 12 | 8 |

*Source: General Household Survey, Office for National Statistics*

# 1.16

## Divorce: by duration of marriage

| United Kingdom | | | | | Percentages |
| --- | --- | --- | --- | --- | --- |
| | 1961 | 1971 | 1981 | 1991 | 1995 |
| 0-2 years | 1 | 1 | 2 | 9 | 9 |
| 3-4 years | 10 | 12 | 19 | 14 | 13 |
| 5-9 years | 31 | 31 | 29 | 27 | 28 |
| 10-14 years | 23 | 19 | 20 | 18 | 18 |
| 15-19 years | } 14 | { 13 | 13 | 13 | 12 |
| 20-24 years | | { 10 | 9 | 10 | 9 |
| 25-29 years | } 21 | { 6 | 5 | 5 | 6 |
| 30 years and over | | { 9 | 5 | 4 | 5 |
| All durations (=100%) | | | | | |
| (thousands) | 27.0 | 79.2 | 155.6 | 171.1 | 170.0 |

*Source: Office for National Statistics; General Register Office for Scotland; Northern Ireland Statistics and Research Agency*

More recent marriages have a greater likelihood of resulting in separation within five years. In addition, women who were under 20 when they married are more likely to separate than women who married at older ages. For example, one in ten marriages entered into by teenage women in Great Britain between 1965 and 1969 ended in separation within five years compared with one in three of similar marriages that took place between 1985 and 1989 (Table 1.15). Marriages by 25 to 29 year old women were more likely to last five years but again a much greater proportion of more recent marriages ended in separation; 8 per cent of these marriages which took place between 1985 and 1989 resulted in separation within five years compared with 2 per cent of those which took place between 1965 and 1969.

The number of divorces in the United Kingdom more than trebled between 1969 and 1994, although in 1994 there were slightly fewer divorces than in the previous year (see Chart 1.11). The *Divorce Reform Act 1969* attempted to remove the concepts of guilty party and matrimonial offence by introducing a solitary ground for divorce, that of irretrievable breakdown of marriage. This could be established by proving one or more of certain facts; adultery, unreasonable behaviour, desertion, two years' separation and five years' separation. The first of these three facts were the so-called former matrimonial offences which were retained with minor changes. The separation facts however were new and undoubtedly demonstrated the fault-free principle more clearly. These allowed divorce to be petitioned for solely by the petitioner, or by mutual consent, after a minimum interval from the date of marriage breakdown. These meant that many petitioners who filed for five years' separation after the Act came into force in 1971 would have been unable to divorce under the old legislation. The number of divorces rose dramatically in 1971 and 1972, which to some extent can be explained by a backlog of cases.

The *Matrimonial and Family Proceedings Act 1984*, which reduced the minimum period after marriage that a petition for divorce could be filed, also had an immediate effect on divorce proceedings in England and Wales. The new law allowed couples to file for divorce after their first wedding anniversary whereas under former legislation they could not usually petition for divorce unless their marriage had lasted at least three years. In 1995, 9 per cent of divorces in the United Kingdom were of marriages that had lasted under three years compared with only 2 per cent in 1981 (Table 1.16).

An analysis has been carried out by the Office for National Statistics to estimate the proportion of marriages that would end in divorce assuming that divorce rates by duration were to persist at their 1993 and 1994 levels. The results indicate that two in

# 1.17

five marriages would ultimately end in divorce and just under half of married couples would celebrate their silver wedding. It has also been calculated that recent marriages, on average, would last about 26 years.

Recent data suggest that the trend in increasing divorce rates per thousand married couples may have levelled out and this seems most evident in the younger age groups. In 1995 divorce rates in England and Wales were highest for men and women in the 25 to 29 age group, but in both cases were lower than the rates in 1991 (Table 1.17). Men had lower divorce rates than women in the age groups under 30, reflecting the age differences between the genders at marriage.

Women were granted almost two and a half times as many divorces as men overall in England, Wales and Northern Ireland in 1995: 110 thousand were granted to women compared with 47 thousand to men and under a thousand to both. This is largely the result of women petitioning for divorce in much greater numbers than men and in most cases the divorce is granted to the petitioner. The most common reason for women to be granted divorce was the unreasonable behaviour of their husbands; for men it was the adultery of their wives (Chart 1.18).

Unreasonable behaviour is the most common reason given by wives of all ages. However, the older the wife is at divorce, the more likely the divorce is to be granted by proving adultery or after two years' separation. However, the proportion granted for these two facts falls for women in their late forties and fifties and separation after five years becomes relatively more common. Jointly awarded divorces have been excluded from the analysis in Chart 1.18.

**Divorce: by gender and age**

| England & Wales | | | | | Rates per 1,000 married population |
|---|---|---|---|---|---|
| | 1961 | 1971 | 1981 | 1991 | 1995 |
| **Males** | | | | | |
| 16-24 | 1.4 | 5.0 | 17.7 | 25.9 | 25.8 |
| 25-29 | 3.9 | 12.5 | 27.6 | 32.9 | 29.4 |
| 30-34 | 4.1 | 11.8 | 22.8 | 28.5 | 28.6 |
| 35-44 | 3.1 | 7.9 | 17.0 | 20.1 | 21.0 |
| 45 and over | 1.1 | 3.1 | 4.8 | 5.6 | 6.2 |
| | | | | | |
| All aged 16 and over | 2.1 | 5.9 | 11.9 | 13.6 | 13.5 |
| **Females** | | | | | |
| 16-24 | 2.4 | 7.5 | 22.3 | 27.7 | 28.3 |
| 25-29 | 4.5 | 13.0 | 26.7 | 31.3 | 30.1 |
| 30-34 | 3.8 | 10.5 | 20.2 | 25.1 | 26.6 |
| 35-44 | 2.7 | 6.7 | 14.9 | 17.2 | 18.6 |
| 45 and over | 0.9 | 2.8 | 3.9 | 4.5 | 5.0 |
| | | | | | |
| All aged 16 and over | 2.1 | 5.9 | 11.9 | 13.4 | 13.4 |

*Source: Office for National Statistics*

# 1.18

**Divorces granted: by fact proven, 1995**

**England, Wales & Northern Ireland**
Thousands

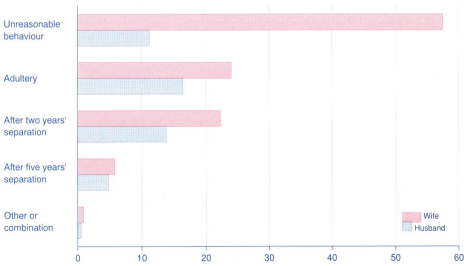

*Source: Office for National Statistics; Northern Ireland Statistics and Research Agency*

# 1.19

## Characteristics of couples who divorced in 1994

| England & Wales | Percentages |
| --- | --- |
| | 1994 |
| **Divorced couples** | |
| With children under 16 | 56 |
| With children aged 16 or over | 14 |
| No children | 31 |
| | |
| All divorced couples | |
| (=100%)(thousands) | 158.2 |
| | |
| **Children[1] of divorced couples** | |
| Aged 0-4 | 31 |
| Aged 5-10 | 43 |
| Aged 11-15 | 27 |
| | |
| All children[1] (=100%)(thousands) | 164.8 |

1 Aged under 16.

**Source: Office for National Statistics**

In many instances children are also affected by divorce. Seven out of ten couples who divorced in England and Wales in 1994 had children (Table 1.19). Of further concern is the fact that the majority of these cases of family breakdown involved children under the age of 16. Almost 165 thousand children were in families that had divorced in 1994. Of these, three in ten children were under five years old and over seven in ten were under ten years of age.

Most people who separate do eventually remarry. For example, among women aged 16 to 59 in Great Britain who were under 35 when their first marriage ended in separation between 1967 and 1970, two thirds had remarried within ten years of their separation (Chart 1.20). However, the likelihood of remarriage after separation appears to be decreasing: 60 per cent of women who separated between 1967 and 1970 had remarried within eight years, but less than half of those separated 12 years later had remarried within the same period. Men are more likely than women to remarry following separation.

When people in Great Britain were interviewed in the 1994 BSA, they were asked if they thought that discontented couples should stay together for the sake of the children. About one in five respondents agreed with the statement that 'when there are children in the family, parents should stay together even if they don't get along'. In contrast, just one in twenty agreed that 'even when there are no children, a married couple should stay together even if they don't get along'.

There are several organisations that offer services for separating and divorcing couples. One of these is National Family Mediation (NFM) which was formed in 1981. NFM co-ordinates the work of around 70 local services in England and Wales. These offer help when a couple who are, or are about to be, separated or divorced disagree over important issues, especially those concerning the children. Family Mediation Scotland provide similar services in Scotland.

NFM take referrals from the courts, solicitors, GPs, social workers, Relate, Citizens Advice Bureaux and other helping agencies, but also accept requests from couples themselves, either individually or jointly. An impartial third person then meets those involved in family breakdown in an informal atmosphere with the aim of

# 1.20

## Women remarrying[1]: by year, and length, of separation, 1994-1996[2]

**Great Britain**

Percentages

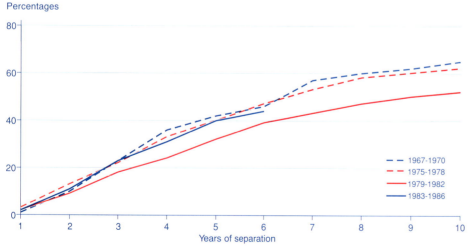

Years of separation

Legend:
- – – 1967-1970
- – – 1975-1978 (red dashed)
- —— 1979-1982 (red)
- —— 1983-1986 (blue)

1 Cumulative percentage of women aged 16 to 59 who were under 35 when their first marriage ended in separation and who had remarried.
2 Combined years: 1994-95 and 1995-96.

**Source: General Household Survey, Office for National Statistics**

# 1.21

reducing conflict and improving communication between the individuals concerned. In particular, they work towards establishing and maintaining a good relationship between both parents and their children and attempt to form a jointly agreed plan for the future, focused on the needs of the children. This is in line with the *Children Act 1989* that states that each parent shall have parental responsibility for the child, even after divorce.

In 1995 around 16 thousand approaches for help were made to NFM services by families in England, Wales and Northern Ireland and over 6 thousand couples engaged in mediation - more than three times the number in 1987. Of those using these services just over two out of three couples resolved all, or some, of the issues during their mediation (Chart 1.21).

The *Family Law Act 1996*, which will come into effect once the administrative details have been put in place, will ensure the even greater use of mediation by couples. It states that the facts required to prove divorce under previous legislation will no longer need to be cited and stipulates that a couple will have a period of reflection and consideration to last a year, or 18 months if children under the age of 16 arc involved. This period will be initiated by attendance at an 'information meeting' followed by a sworn statement that one or both parties believe the marriage to have irretrievably broken down. The couple will then be encouraged to use mediation to make their arrangements and resolve any disputes before the divorce is granted. The purpose of this is to try to reduce the suffering caused by family breakdown.

## Family building

Most women have children at some stage in their lives; 83 per cent of women who were born in 1954 in England and Wales had had at least one child by their fortieth birthday. However, changes in marriage, cohabitation and divorce patterns, as well as social and economic factors, have had a significant effect on family building trends.

Chart 1.22 shows the average number of children born to women of different ages in England and Wales by their year of birth. There has been a fall in the average number of children per woman for women born in successive decades since 1935. For example, by the age of 25, women born in 1945 had had, on average, 1.2 children whereas women born 20 years later had had only 0.7 children by the same age.

## Outcome of family mediation, 1995

**England, Wales & Northern Ireland**
Percentages

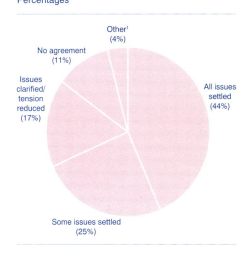

1 Cases where either the people concerned were reconciled or where the outcome was unclear.
*Source: National Family Mediation*

# 1.22

## Average number of children born to women by certain ages: by year of birth, and age, of mother, 1995

**England & Wales**
Children per woman

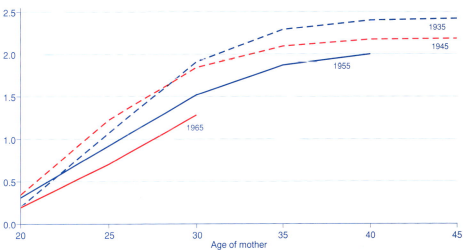

*Source: Office for National Statistics*

# 1.23

### Mean age of mother for births inside marriage, 1991 and 1995

| England & Wales | | Years |
| --- | --- | --- |
| | 1991 | 1995 |
| First birth | 27.5 | 28.5 |
| Second birth | 28.9 | 30.0 |
| Third birth | 30.4 | 31.1 |
| Fourth birth | 31.6 | 32.0 |
| All births inside marriage | 28.9 | 29.8 |

*Source: Office for National Statistics*

There has also been a decline in the average number of children born to women by the age of 40, which is near the end of their child-bearing years. By the age of 40 women who were born in 1935 had an average of 2.4 children, compared with 2.0 for women born in 1955.

While the average number of children born to women has declined, there has been a distinct trend towards women deferring their child-bearing to older ages. Fertility rates for women in their twenties have fallen since the peak in the mid 1960s as more and more women have delayed starting their families until their thirties. In 1992, for the first time ever, women in their early thirties were more likely to have a baby than women in their early twenties. There have also been increases in the fertility rates of women in their late thirties and early forties over the last 15 years. However, women aged 25 to 29 are still the most likely to give birth - with a rate of 107 births per thousand women in 1996.

The average age of women giving birth over the last 20 years or so has consistently risen - mothers in 1996 were, on average, two years older than those giving birth in 1976. Some of the reasons for this delay in child-bearing are thought to be similar to those for the increase in the average age at marriage, such as the greater participation of women in higher education. The increasing proportion of women who continue working and want to develop their career before starting a family and the greater choice and effectiveness of contraceptive methods, which have increasingly enabled women to choose when to have children and how many to have, have also contributed.

Not surprisingly, the average age of married women when they have their first child within marriage has also increased. This rose by one year between 1991 and 1995, from 27.5 years to 28.5 years for women in England and Wales (Table 1.23). During this period the average age at each successive birth also increased, but at successively slower rates. Births that occur outside marriage are usually to younger mothers than those which occur inside marriage. The average age of women at childbirth outside marriage was 26.0 years in 1995, whereas the average age of women giving birth within marriage was 29.8 years.

# 1.24

### Median interval between marriage and first birth[1]: by social class of father

| England & Wales | | | | Months |
| --- | --- | --- | --- | --- |
| | 1971 | 1975 | 1985 | 1995 |
| Professional, managerial and technical | 29 | 37 | 37 | 33 |
| Skilled non-manual | 26 | 35 | 33 | 30 |
| Skilled manual | 19 | 25 | 26 | 27 |
| Semi-skilled and unskilled manual | 13 | 18 | 18 | 25 |
| All social classes | 20 | 28 | 28 | 29 |

*1 To women married only once.*
*Source: Office for National Statistics*

The rate of multiple births has also risen over the past decade, from 10.4 per thousand maternities in 1985 to 14.1 per thousand maternities in 1995. This is important because of the health and social care implications for the families involved. While infant mortality rates for multiple births have declined, they remain higher than those for single births and babies of multiple maternities also often require intensive care treatment. It has also been recognised that caring for twins, triplets and higher order births can put families under financial and emotional strain. The greater use of fertility treatments and increasing average age of women giving birth have been important factors in the rise of the rate of multiple births. Older women are more likely to have non-identical twins, in particular, than younger women. For women in their late thirties, multiple births accounted for just over 20 in every thousand maternities in England and Wales in 1995. This compares with fewer than seven in every thousand maternities for women aged under 20.

The proportion of first births within marriage occurring within the first year of marriage in England and Wales fell from 24 per cent in 1985 to 20 per cent in 1995. This partly reflects the fact that women have become much more likely to have children outside marriage or have an abortion than to have a 'shotgun' wedding. The median interval between marriage and first birth within marriage to women married once only increased from 20 months in 1971 to 29 months in 1995 (Table 1.24). However, nearly all of this increase took place between 1971 and 1975 and there was little change thereafter.

The median interval between marriage and first birth within marriage does vary according to the social class of the father. There has been a reduction in the median interval length for those in the non-manual classes between 1975 and 1995, while for the manual classes it continued to rise. Despite this, those in the non-manual classes still take longer after marrying to have their first child than those in the manual classes.

**Births outside marriage as a percentage of all live births**

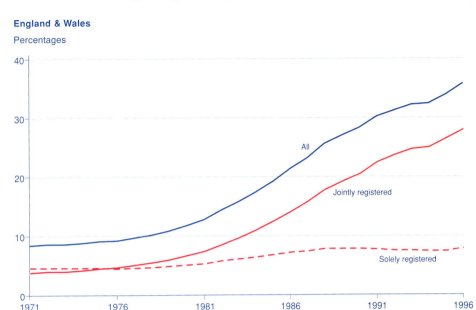

**England & Wales**

Percentages

*Source: Office for National Statistics*

Most children are born to married couples, although this proportion has declined over the last few decades. Over a third of all live births were outside marriage in England and Wales in 1996, which was more than four times the proportion in 1971 (Chart 1.25). The rise in this proportion was particularly steep in the 1980s but may have slowed in more recent years.

Despite the increase in births outside of marriage, there is evidence to suggest that most of these births occur to mothers who have a partner. Around four fifths of births outside marriage were jointly registered by both parents in 1995, of which the large majority were living at the same address. Births outside of marriage that were solely registered were particularly common to mothers in the younger age groups. In 1995, four fifths of solely registered births were to women aged under 30 compared with half of all births within marriage.

# 1.26

## Dependent children: by family type

| Great Britain | | | | Percentages |
|---|---|---|---|---|
| | 1972 | 1981 | 1991-92 | 1995-96 |
| **Couples** | | | | |
| 1 child | 16 | 18 | 17 | 16 |
| 2 children | 35 | 41 | 37 | 38 |
| 3 or more children | 41 | 29 | 28 | 26 |
| **Lone mothers** | | | | |
| 1 child | 2 | 3 | 5 | 5 |
| 2 children | 2 | 4 | 7 | 7 |
| 3 or more children | 2 | 3 | 6 | 6 |
| **Lone fathers** | | | | |
| 1 child | - | 1 | - | 1 |
| 2 or more children | 1 | 1 | 1 | 1 |
| **All dependent children** | 100 | 100 | 100 | 100 |

*Source: General Household Survey, Office for National Statistics*

# 1.27

## Families with dependent children: by age of youngest child, 1995-96

| Great Britain | | | | | Percentages |
|---|---|---|---|---|---|
| | 0-4 | 5-9 | 10-15 | 16 and over | All ages |
| **Couples** | | | | | |
| Married | 40 | 26 | 26 | 7 | 100 |
| Cohabiting | 63 | 19 | 15 | 2 | 100 |
| **Lone parents** | | | | | |
| Lone mothers | 36 | 34 | 23 | 7 | 100 |
| Lone fathers | 6 | 21 | 56 | 17 | 100 |
| **All families with dependent children** | 40 | 27 | 26 | 7 | 100 |

*Source: General Household Survey, Office for National Statistics*

The Longitudinal Study has been used to assess change in the family status of children in families. Links have been made between the birth registration records of children aged under ten in England and Wales and their family status according to the 1991 Census. It found that children born within marriage are more likely to still be living with their natural parents than those born outside marriage, even if their birth was registered jointly by the mother and father.

## Parenting

The majority of children grow up in a family with two parents; four fifths of dependent children lived in such families in Great Britain in 1995-96 (Table 1.26). However, this proportion has fallen since 1972 when over nine tenths of children lived in a couple family. Most children are also brought up in a family with other children; almost four fifths of dependent children lived with at least one other dependent child in 1995-96.

Although the proportion of children in couple families with three or more children declined during the 1970s, it has remained relatively stable since the early 1980s. In 1995-96 just over a quarter of dependent children lived in a family with three or more children. In Northern Ireland a higher proportion, almost two fifths, of children lived in these larger families. It is now more common for children to be brought up in lone parent families, with 20 per cent of dependent children living in such families in Great Britain in 1995-96 compared with 7 per cent in 1972.

# 1.28

The average number of dependent children in families with dependent children is slightly higher for married couples than for lone parents. Married couples had an average of 1.9 children per family and lone parents had an average of 1.7 children in 1995-96 in Great Britain. The overall average number of children in families with dependent children fell from 2.0 in 1971 to 1.8 in 1981 but has not changed over the last 15 years.

There is some variation however in the age of the youngest dependent child in different types of family in Great Britain. In 1995-96, over three fifths of cohabiting couples with dependent children had a child under the age of four compared with two fifths of married couples and a third of lone parent families with dependent children (Table 1.27). Lone fathers with dependent children were least likely to have young children and this can be largely accounted for when the reasons why they became lone fathers are considered.

An analysis of the marital status of lone parents gives a good indication of the causes of lone parenthood. In the period 1994-95 to 1995-96, just 8 per cent of lone fathers were single (that is, had never married) compared with 38 per cent of lone mothers (Table 1.28). Lone fathers were much more likely to be divorced, widowed or separated than lone mothers and this explains why they tend to have older children than lone mothers and couple families.

There has been substantial growth in lone parent families over the last 25 years. Lone parents headed 22 per cent of all families with dependent children in Great Britain in 1995, which was nearly three times the proportion in 1971 although this may have levelled off in recent years (Chart 1.29). This increase was almost totally due to the dramatic rise in the proportion of lone mothers while the proportion of lone fathers has remained relatively constant throughout the period. The growth in the number of lone mothers up to the mid 1980s was mainly due to the increase in the number of women with children divorcing, brought about not only by more divorce but also by a decline in remarriage. Since 1986 the most substantial

### Lone parents: by gender and marital status, 1994-1996[1]

| Great Britain | | Percentages |
| --- | --- | --- |
| | Lone mothers | Lone fathers |
| Single | 38 | 8 |
| Divorced | 34 | 49 |
| Separated | 23 | 29 |
| Widowed | 5 | 13 |
| All lone parents | 100 | 100 |

1 Combined years: 1994-95 and 1995-96.

*Source: General Household Survey, Office for National Statistics*

# 1.29

### Families headed by lone parents as a percentage[1] of all families with dependent children

**Great Britain**

Percentages

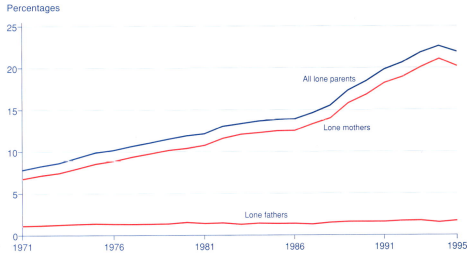

1 Three year moving average used (apart from 1994 and 1995).

*Source: General Household Survey, Office for National Statistics*

# 1.30

## Lone parents: by gender and age, 1994-1996[1]

| Great Britain | | Percentages |
|---|---|---|
| | Lone mothers | Lone fathers |
| 16-24 | 14 | 1 |
| 25-29 | 19 | 2 |
| 30-34 | 24 | 7 |
| 35-39 | 18 | 26 |
| 40-44 | 13 | 33 |
| 45-49 | 8 | 19 |
| 50-54 | 3 | 9 |
| 55-59 | 1 | 2 |
| 60 and over | - | 1 |
| All aged 16 and over | 100 | 100 |

1 Combined years: 1994-95 and 1995-96.

**Source: General Household Survey, Office for National Statistics**

# 1.31

## Changes each year to lone parent families with dependent children: by gender, 1991-1995

| Great Britain | | | Percentages |
|---|---|---|---|
| | Lone mothers | Lone fathers | All |
| **Status at end of each year** | | | |
| Still lone parent | 85 | 75 | 84 |
| Married or cohabiting | 11 | 9 | 11 |
| Dependent children no longer present | - | 6 | 1 |
| Children no longer dependent | 4 | 11 | 4 |
| All | 100 | 100 | 100 |

**Source: British Household Panel Survey, ESRC Research Centre on Micro-social Change**

growth has been among never-married lone mothers, some of whom will have experienced the breakdown of a cohabiting union. Most lone parent families with dependent children are therefore headed by a lone mother. In 1995 there were 12 lone mothers to every lone father while lone fathers accounted for less than 2 per cent of all families with dependent children.

The age distribution of lone mothers and fathers is also very different. Table 1.27 indicated that lone fathers with dependent children were more likely to have older children. It is therefore not surprising that lone fathers tend to be older than lone mothers - almost two thirds of lone fathers in Great Britain were aged 40 or over in the period 1994-95 to 1995-96 (Table 1.30). In contrast, of the much larger number of lone mothers, a quarter were aged 40 or over while a third of them were under the age of 30.

An analysis of the BHPS found that in the early 1990s, on average, around one in six lone parents each year ceased to be lone parents (Table 1.31). The study estimated that, if such a departure rate was maintained over time, over half of all lone parents would have a duration of lone parenthood of around four years or less. There are once again differences between lone mothers and fathers. Lone fathers were less likely to still be a lone father a year later. This is because they generally have older children who are more likely to either have moved out of the household to live elsewhere or no longer be dependent on their father one year later. The main reason that a lone mother ceases to be a lone parent is because she has formed a new partnership.

In 1995 the BSA asked people about their attitudes to unmarried mothers. Almost a third of respondents agreed with the statement that 'unmarried mothers who find it hard to cope have only themselves to blame', while just over a quarter agreed that 'unmarried mothers get too little sympathy from society'. Nearly two thirds of people agreed that a single mother should receive some money from the government for childcare if she got a part-time job (see also Table 2.7).

When lone parents form new partnerships step-families may be created. These can be either married, or cohabiting, couples with dependent children living in their family, one or more of whom are not the natural children of both the man and woman. Information on step-families, where the head of the family was aged under 60, is available from the General Household Survey. In 1991-92 there were about half a million step-families with dependent children in Great Britain with over 1 million dependent children living in such families. This meant that about 7 per cent of children lived in step-families, which was slightly higher than the 5 per cent in 1979. Families containing step-children tend to be larger than families with natural children only. In married couple step-families there were, on average, 2.3 dependent children in 1991-92 compared with 1.9 in married couple families with only natural children.

In the period 1991-92 to 1992-93, step-families with dependent children accounted for just over 7 per cent of all families with dependent children where the head was aged under 60 (Table 1.32). Most step-families with dependent children, over two thirds, are headed by married couples. However, the third that are headed by cohabiting couples indicates a higher level of cohabitation by step-parents than among families where both natural parents are present. It should be noted that step-families can also contain non-dependent children only and these made up about 1 per cent of all families in Great Britain.

There is a tendency for children to remain with their mother after a partnership breaks up. In 90 per cent of step-families in 1995-96, at least one child was from a previous relationship of the woman. This compares with 14 per cent of step-families where there was at least one child from the man's previous relationship. In 4 per cent of step-families, therefore, there were children from both partners' previous relationships.

Sometimes children are adopted by a step-parent or are adopted into a family that does not include either of their natural parents. Families with adopted children, however, are now quite rare. The number of adoptions in Great Britain peaked in 1968, at 27 thousand. Since then it has fallen substantially so that the total of just over 6 thousand adoptions in 1995 was less than a quarter of the number in 1968. There were particularly large falls in 1976 and 1977 just after the first few sections of the *Children Act* were implemented.

The use of contraception, the increase in abortions and changes in attitudes towards lone parenthood have also contributed to the fall in the number of children available for adoption. These factors also help explain the trend towards adoption of older children. Just 6 per cent of children who were adopted in 1995 were under the age of one (Chart 1.33) compared with 51 per cent in 1968. Almost a third of children who were adopted in 1995 were aged ten or over.

### Stepfamilies and families with dependent children[1], 1991-1993[2]

| Great Britain | Percentages |
|---|---|
| | 1991-1993[2] |
| **Married couple stepfamilies** | |
| Stepfather/natural mother | 4.3 |
| Stepmother/natural father | 0.5 |
| Stepfather/stepmother | 0.2 |
| All married couple stepfamilies | 5.0 |
| **Cohabiting couple stepfamilies** | |
| Stepfather/natural mother | 2.0 |
| Stepmother/natural father | 0.2 |
| Stepfather/stepmother | 0.1 |
| All cohabiting couple stepfamilies | 2.3 |
| **Lone parent families** | 20.9 |
| **Couple families with natural children only** | 71.8 |
| **All families with dependent children** | 100.0 |

1 Families with dependent children whose family head is aged 16 to 59.
2 Combined years: 1991-92 and 1992-93.
**Source: General Household Survey, Office for National Statistics**

# 1.33

### Adoptions: by age of child, 1995

**Great Britain**
Percentages

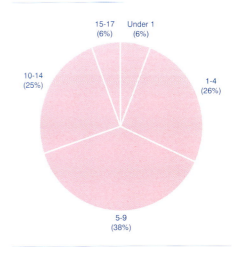

15-17 (6%)  Under 1 (6%)
10-14 (25%)
1-4 (26%)
5-9 (38%)

**Source: Office for National Statistics; General Register Office for Scotland**

# 1.34

**Foster placements: by age of child, 1995[1]**

| England & Wales | Percentages |
|---|---|
| | 1995[1] |
| Under 1 | 4 |
| 1-4 | 15 |
| 5-9 | 23 |
| 10-15 | 43 |
| 16-17 | 15 |
| 18 and over | 1 |
| | |
| All foster placements (=100%) (thousands) | 32.9 |

1 At 31 March 1995.

**Source: Department of Health; Welsh Office**

Some children and young people are looked after by local authorities. At 31 March 1995, just over 50 thousand children were being looked after by the local authorities in England and Wales and almost two thirds of these were in foster placements. This proportion has been increasing gradually over the last ten years as fewer children are being placed elsewhere, in particular in community homes. In 1985 only half of children looked after by local authorities were in foster placements.

Foster children tend to be older than adopted children - almost three in five foster children were aged ten or over compared with just one in five under the age of five in 1995 (Table 1.34). Only one in seven foster children were placed with a relative or friend but over four fifths were placed within the same local authority that was responsible for their care so that they were at least familiar with the area in which they were living and often had relatives and friends near them.

# 2

# Family living standards

## Economic activity

The diversification of family structures witnessed over the last few decades has been accompanied by some major changes in the economic characteristics of families. Employment is the main means by which families support themselves financially and plays a pivotal role in the way they lead their lives. The worlds of work and family are often interdependent. Work can impact on family life by limiting the time available for being with family members and for carrying out family duties and, conversely, family responsibilities may act as a constraint on labour market participation.

A fundamental change in the structure of the labour market over the last few decades has been the increased participation of women, particularly the extent to which they have taken up part-time work. The proportion of women of working age in Great Britain who were in employment increased from 59 per cent in Spring 1979 to 67 per cent in Spring 1996. Women represented 44 per cent of the labour force of working age by the end of this period. Not surprisingly, this trend has had a considerable impact on women's role in the family.

# Economic activity

## 2.1

### Married couples[1] with dependent children: by number of earners

**Great Britain**

Percentages

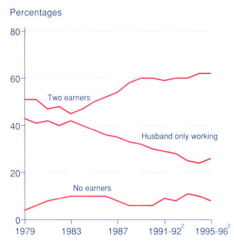

1 Males aged 16 to 64 and females aged 16 to 59.
2 Financial years after 1987.

*Source: General Household Survey, Office for National Statistics*

The increasing proportion of women entering the labour market, continuing to work after marriage and returning to employment after childbirth has meant that the traditional family model of 'breadwinner husband and homemaker wife' is less common. Indeed, the most significant change in the working patterns of families has been the fall in the number of families living solely on a man's wages, and the related increase in the number of dual earner families.

In just over three in five married couple families of working age with dependent children both adults were in employment in Great Britain in 1995-96 compared with around a half in the early 1980s (Chart 2.1). In contrast, the proportion of families where only the husband was working fell from around two in five in the early 1980s to just over a quarter in 1995-96. There has been an increase in the proportion of families with dependent children where only the wife is working. However, this is still quite rare and only 4 per cent of such families were in this position in 1995-96.

Results from the British Social Attitudes Survey (BSA) show that support for the traditional gender roles is declining. In 1994, 24 per cent of respondents agreed with the statement that 'a husband's job is to earn money; a wife's job is to look after the home and family' compared with 43 per cent in 1984. The 1994 BSA also indicated that women were more likely to disagree with the statement than men.

The economic activity status (see box on page 31) of working age couples in the United Kingdom in Autumn 1996 is shown in Table 2.2. In over three quarters of the families where the head of the family was working, their partner was also working. However, where the head of the family was not working, in just over three fifths of these couples the partner was not working either. These patterns are largely determined by local labour market conditions, but also reflect the tendency of men and women with similar qualifications and work backgrounds to form partnerships.

Not surprisingly, having dependent children has quite an impact on the working arrangements of couples. Although the partners in these families were only slightly less likely to be working than if they did not have children, they were much more likely to be working part time. Where both the head and the partner in a family with dependent children were working, the partner was working part time in just over three fifths of cases. This is probably because many women with family responsibilities find working part time more convenient.

## 2.2

### Economic activity status of couples[1], Autumn 1996

**United Kingdom**                                                                              Percentages

|  | Head of family | | | | |
|---|---|---|---|---|---|
|  | Working full time | Working part time | Unemp-loyed[2] | Inactive | All |
| **Partner** | | | | | |
| Working full time | 33.2 | 1.1 | 0.9 | 2.0 | 37.2 |
| Working part time | 30.6 | 1.2 | 0.8 | 1.7 | 34.2 |
| Unemployed[2] | 2.2 | 0.1 | 0.6 | 0.3 | 3.2 |
| Inactive | | | | | |
| Looking after family/home | 10.8 | 0.7 | 1.9 | 2.7 | 16.1 |
| Other inactive | 5.3 | 0.4 | 0.8 | 2.8 | 9.3 |
| All | 82.1 | 3.5 | 4.9 | 9.5 | 100.0 |

1 Males aged 16 to 64 and females aged 16 to 59.
2 Based on the ILO definition.

*Source: Labour Force Survey, Office for National Statistics*

# 2.3

It is the age of the youngest child rather than the number of children that is the major factor in the participation of the mother in the labour market. As the age of the youngest child increases, mothers are increasingly likely to be in employment and, in particular, are more likely to be in full-time work (Table 2.3). However, although mothers with children aged under five are the least likely to be in paid work, it is this group of women who have experienced the greatest increase in labour market participation over the last decade.

The Family and Working Lives Survey (FWLS), which was carried out between July 1994 and February 1995 in Great Britain, asked couples with children whether the presence of their children had affected their working arrangements. Around two thirds of female partners, but only a sixth of male partners, said that it had. Female partners said that their hours and type of work had been affected and one in ten specifically mentioned missing out on promotion. Male partners also mentioned some constraints, such as having to take the children to school or not being able to work away from home. However, the impact of having children on their working arrangements was small compared with the impact for female partners.

The FWLS also asked mothers whether they had returned to work within a year of the birth of their first child. Generally, the more recent generation of mothers was more likely to have returned to work within a year than the earlier one. For example, 37 per cent of mothers who were aged 25 to 34 at the time of interview said that they had returned to work within a year of the birth of their first child compared with 14 per cent of mothers aged 60 to 64 (Chart 2.4).

**Economic activity status of mothers[1]: by age of youngest child, Spring 1996**

United Kingdom  
Percentages

|  | Age of youngest child | | | All mothers[1] |
|---|---|---|---|---|
|  | 0-4 | 5-10 | 11-15 |  |
| Working full time | 17 | 22 | 34 | 22 |
| Working part time | 31 | 43 | 41 | 37 |
| Unemployed[2] | 5 | 5 | 4 | 5 |
| Inactive | 46 | 30 | 21 | 35 |
| All mothers[1] (=100%)(millions) | 3.1 | 2.2 | 1.5 | 6.8 |

1 Mothers aged 16 to 59 with children aged under 16.
2 Based on the ILO definition.
**Source: Labour Force Survey, Office for National Statistics**

**Economically active:** people who are employees, self-employed, participants in government employment and training programmes, doing unpaid family work, and those who are unemployed on the ILO definition.
**Economically inactive:** people who are neither in employment nor ILO unemployed.

**ILO unemployed:** the International Labour Organisation (ILO) recommended measure, which counts as unemployed those aged 16 and over who are without a job, are available to start work in the next two weeks and who have been seeking a job in the last four weeks or are waiting to start a job already obtained.

# 2.4

**Mothers who returned to work within one year of the birth of their first child: by age[1], 1994-95[2]**

**Great Britain**  
Percentages

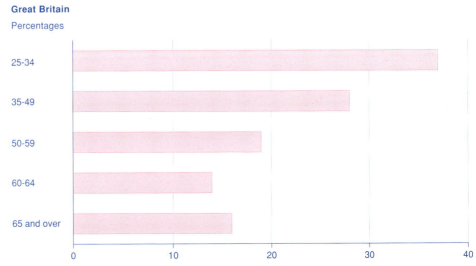

1 Age of mother at time of interview.
2 Main fieldwork took place between July 1994 and February 1995.
**Source: Family and Working Lives Survey, Department for Education and Employment**

# 2.5

## Attitudes[1] towards mothers working, 1994

**Great Britain**                                                                 Percentages

|  | Should work full time | Should work part time | Should stay at home | Can't choose/not answered | All |
|---|---|---|---|---|---|
| After marrying and before there are children | 80 | 9 | 2 | 9 | 100 |
| When there is a child under school age | 5 | 28 | 55 | 11 | 100 |
| After the youngest child starts school | 16 | 65 | 8 | 11 | 100 |
| After the children leave home | 63 | 21 | 2 | 15 | 100 |

1 People aged 18 and over were asked: 'Do you think that women should work outside the home full time, part time or not at all under these circumstances?'.

**Source: British Social Attitudes Survey, Social & Community Planning Research**

# 2.6

## Childcare arrangements used by mothers[1] who are employees: by age of youngest child, 1994

**Great Britain**                                                                 Percentages

|  | Age of youngest child | | |
|---|---|---|---|
|  | 0-4 | 5-11 | All[1] |
| Relative[2] | 69 | 57 | 62 |
| Mother works only while children are at school | 7 | 37 | 23 |
| Childminder | 25 | 7 | 15 |
| Friend/neighbour | 3 | 23 | 13 |
| Day nursery | 14 | - | 6 |
| Mother's help/nanny | 9 | 3 | 6 |
| Mother works at/from home | 2 | 6 | 4 |
| Children look after themselves | - | 8 | 4 |
| Workplace nursery | 2 | 1 | 2 |

1 Employees aged 16 to 59 with children aged under 12 who work more than 10 hours a week. Percentages add to more than 100 as respondents were asked to mention all the arrangements they used.
2 Includes husband or partner.

**Source: British Social Attitudes Survey, Social & Community Planning Research**

Just over three fifths of the mothers who returned to work within a year of the birth of their first child returned to work for the same employer. The higher the qualifications a mother held, the more likely she was to return to the same employer. Seven out of ten mothers with higher education qualifications who returned to work went back to the same employer compared with around half of mothers with no qualifications.

The most common reasons which mothers gave for returning to work were finance-related. Over a half gave at least one financial reason for returning to work such as earning money to buy basic essentials or extras and one income in the family not being enough. However, at least a quarter also gave one or more self-fulfilment reasons for returning to work such as enjoying work and pursuing their career.

The 1994 BSA analysed adults' attitudes towards mothers working. Respondents were asked whether they thought that women should work outside the home full time, part time or not at all according to various family circumstances. Table 2.5 shows that almost nine in ten people agreed that women should go out to work after getting married and the great majority of these thought that they should work full time. In contrast, over half of people thought mothers of pre-school children should stay at home. Of those who thought that a mother should work, all but a small minority thought it should be part time only.

Once the youngest child has started school, it appears to be more acceptable for a mother to work. Four out of five people thought such mothers should work but again most of these thought that it should be part time. Full-time employment was endorsed by the majority of people for mothers with children who had left home; over three fifths thought that this was the best option.

When mothers of pre-school children return to work, some form of childcare has to be arranged. While childcare requirements are lessened when children start nursery or primary school, there still remains the need to cover school holidays and the gaps between the start and end of an adult's working day. In 1994 mothers who were employees with children under the age of 12 were asked how they arranged for their children to be looked after while they were at work (Table 2.6). Most working mothers, especially those with pre-school children, did not go beyond the confines of the extended family in arranging childcare. Just over three in five said that a relative or their partner looked after their children.

The use of other forms of childcare by working mothers varies according to the age of the youngest child. The second most popular choice for working mothers of pre-school children was a childminder with a quarter of these mothers using this arrangement. For working mothers of older children, working only while their children were at school was quite common. Over a third of working mothers whose youngest child was aged between 5 and 11 worked only while their children were at school.

It should be noted that it is not only mothers in paid work who make use of childcare arrangements. Others may also use some form of childcare for several reasons: to make time for domestic duties; to take part in leisure activities; or to involve their children in educational and social activities. Many fathers share or take the responsibility for caring for their children, but it is still mothers who generally take the lead.

Results from the 1994 BSA show that the majority of working mothers were already using the form of childcare they most preferred and approaching two thirds were 'very satisfied' with these arrangements and found them 'very convenient'. Not surprisingly, therefore, two out of three mothers in work said that they would work the same amount of hours even if they had the childcare arrangement of their choice. However, when asked, four out of five non-working mothers said that they would go to work if they had access to the childcare arrangement of their choice. This indicates that the lack of suitable childcare arrangements is a major obstacle to some women returning to work.

In 1994 women in Great Britain were asked whether they agreed or disagreed with the statement that 'families should receive financial benefits for childcare when both parents work'. As might be expected, women with children were more likely to favour this suggestion than those without children (Table 2.7). In addition, women overall were more likely to agree with the statement than men.

The majority of working mothers claimed that they would most prefer their partner or another relative to look after their children, an option that is not always available. If this is the case and mothers will not return to work unless their preferred form of childcare is available, then it may be that receiving financial benefits for childcare will not make much difference. In addition, many women also indicated that they would most like to work while their children were at school or take their children to a workplace nursery. Whether these mothers work or not is most likely to be influenced by the availability of suitable part-time jobs and accommodating employers.

**Women's attitudes towards financial benefits for childcare[1]: by presence of children[2] in household, 1994**

| Great Britain | | Percentages |
|---|---|---|
| | Children[2] | No children[2] |
| Strongly agree/agree | 70 | 50 |
| Neither agree nor disagree | 13 | 13 |
| Disagree/strongly disagree | 15 | 31 |
| Can't choose/not answered | 2 | 5 |
| All | 100 | 100 |

1 Women aged 18 and over in the household were asked: 'Should families receive financial benefits for childcare when both parents work?'.
2 Aged under 16.

*Source: British Social Attitudes Survey, Social & Community Planning Research*

# 2.8

## Availability and use of flexible working arrangements by parents[1]: by gender, 1994

**Great Britain**                                                                                    Percentages

|                                  | Fathers | | Mothers | |
|----------------------------------|-----------|------|-----------|------|
|                                  | Available | Use  | Available | Use  |
| Part-time working                | 29        | 6    | 84        | 57   |
| Time off to care for sick children | 49      | 33   | 53        | 41   |
| Flexible hours                   | 39        | 32   | 46        | 38   |
| Job sharing                      | 15        | -    | 33        | 8    |
| Term-time working                | 8         | 3    | 23        | 15   |
| Working at/from home             | 23        | 18   | 16        | 12   |
| School holiday care              | 3         | 1    | 9         | 3    |

1 Male employees aged 16 to 64 and female employees aged 16 to 59 with children aged under 12 who work more than 10 hours a week. Percentages add to more than 100 as respondents were asked to mention all arrangements available to them.
*Source: British Social Attitudes Survey, Social & Community Planning Research*

In 1994 employees of working age with children aged 12 or under in Great Britain were asked about the availability of different flexible working arrangements and, if they were available, whether they used them (Table 2.8). The results indicated that working mothers are much more likely than fathers to work for employers who provide flexible working arrangements. However, a contributing factor may also be that men were less aware that such facilities existed than women.

More than four out of five mothers who were employees had access to part-time working and one in three has access to job-sharing schemes. In contrast, men are not particularly likely to work for an employer that offers flexible working arrangements. However, they are quite likely to use facilities such as taking time off to care for children and paternity leave when they are available. The 1994 BSA also suggested

that employers may have become slightly more flexible as respondents reported a small increase in the provision of some of these working arrangements over the previous four years. For example, the proportion of employees who were able to work flexible hours increased from 30 per cent to 35 per cent over the period.

The total number of hours that people in the United Kingdom work affects how much time they are able to spend with their families. Interestingly, male full-time employees with dependent children work on average two hours longer per week than those without children (Table 2.9). This may be a result of them either being more likely to be at an age where career advancement is critical or needing to work longer hours in order to earn extra money to support their children. In comparison, the average number of hours worked by women was much the same irrespective of whether they had dependent children or no children at all.

The National Child Development Study (NCDS), which interviewed a group of people aged 33 in 1991, examined how parents were managing their different responsibilities as parents and workers. The conclusion was that fathers were often working long hours; two thirds of the fathers were working 40 hours or more a week and over a quarter more than 50 hours a week. It also suggested that where fathers worked significantly more than a 40 hour week, they often participated less in joint family activities. In contrast, the number of hours that mothers spent at work made little difference to their involvement in shared

# 2.9

family activities. Working unsociable hours had less of an effect on family activities than male parents' longer working hours. Two out of three fathers and four out of ten mothers regularly worked evenings or at weekends. The NCDS did suggest though that many couples had successfully adapted to modern working patterns while continuing to find time for their children. Further information on family relationships and activities undertaken by families together is contained in Chapter Three.

**Average hours[1] worked per week: by parental status and gender, Spring 1996**

| United Kingdom | | | | Hours per week |
| --- | --- | --- | --- | --- |
| | Parents[2] | | Non-parents[3] | |
| | Males | Females | Males | Females |
| Working full time | 47.9 | 41.0 | 45.9 | 41.2 |
| Working part time | 19.8 | 18.1 | 16.0 | 17.7 |
| All in employment | 47.1 | 26.9 | 43.0 | 33.7 |

1 Total usual hours including paid and unpaid overtime and excluding meal breaks worked by males aged 16 to 64 and females aged 16 to 59 in employment.
2 With dependent children.
3 Without children.
**Source: Labour Force Survey, Office for National Statistics**

# Income

Income is an important measure of the standard of living of both families and the country as a whole. The level and source of income varies between different families, but is particularly different for retired people who are usually no longer participating in the labour market. For this reason, retired couples have been separated out in most of the income analyses included in this section.

The Family Resources Survey (FRS) and Households Below Average Income (HBAI) analyses are sources of a range of data on the income of the population. Both FRS and HBAI provide statistics on families by classifying individuals into different family types. The definitions of these family types (see box) are on a slightly different basis to the standard definitions that have been used throughout most of this report. In addition most income analyses in this section are based on equivalised income (see box).

**HBAI and FRS family definitions:** HBAI and FRS analyses classify individuals according to the family type of the benefit unit in which they live (regardless of whether they are in receipt of any social security benefits or not). The family types that are used in this section are listed below with their definitions.

*Retired couples*: benefit units headed by couples, where the man of the benefit unit is of state pension age or over.

*Couples with dependent children*: benefit units headed by non-retired couples with dependent children.

*Couples with no dependent children*: benefit units headed by non-retired couples with no dependent children (ie either couples with non-dependent children only or no children).

*Lone parents with dependent children*: benefit units headed by non-retired single adults aged 16 or over with dependent children.

**Equivalised income:** To allow comparisons to be made between the income distributions of families of different types, equivalence scales are used to take account of variations in size and composition of households. These reflect the common-sense notion that a couple family with three dependent children will need a higher income than a couple with no dependent children to have a comparable standard of living.

# 2.10

### Sources of gross household income: by family type, 1994-95

**Great Britain**                                                                                   Percentages

| | Earned income[1] | Non-state pen-sions[2] | Invest-ment income | Means-tested benefits | Non-means-tested benefits | Other sources[3] | Gross household income (=100%) (£ per week) |
|---|---|---|---|---|---|---|---|
| Retired couples | 10 | 31 | 9 | 3 | 45 | 2 | 250 |
| Non-retired couples | | | | | | | |
| Dependent children | 88 | 1 | 1 | 3 | 5 | 1 | 499 |
| No dependent children | 83 | 7 | 3 | 1 | 4 | 2 | 460 |
| Lone parents | | | | | | | |
| Dependent children | 32 | - | - | 44 | 14 | 10 | 190 |
| All families | 75 | 6 | 3 | 5 | 10 | 2 | 405 |

1 Includes wages and salaries and self-employment income.
2 Includes all pensions other than state retirement pension.
3 Includes maintenance, allowances from friends and relatives, private benefits and odd jobs.
**Source: Family Resources Survey, Department of Social Security**

# 2.11

### Percentage of individuals in each quintile group[1]: by family type, 1993-1995[2]

**United Kingdom**                                                                                   Percentages

| | Bottom fifth | Next fifth | Middle fifth | Next fifth | Top fifth | All |
|---|---|---|---|---|---|---|
| Retired couples | 24 | 31 | 21 | 12 | 12 | 100 |
| Non-retired couples | | | | | | |
| Dependent children | 20 | 18 | 24 | 22 | 17 | 100 |
| No dependent children | 10 | 11 | 16 | 26 | 37 | 100 |
| Lone parents | | | | | | |
| Dependent children | 44 | 32 | 14 | 7 | 3 | 100 |
| All individuals[3] | 20 | 20 | 20 | 20 | 20 | 100 |

1 Equivalised household disposable income has been used for ranking all individuals into quintile groups.
2 Combined years: 1993-94 and 1994-95.
3 Includes single people with no dependent children and single retired people as well as individuals in the family types.
**Source: Department of Social Security from Family Expenditure Survey**

Families receive income from many sources. Non-retired couple families had the highest gross income in 1994-95 in Great Britain and this consisted mainly of earnings (Table 2.10). People in retired couples and lone parents with dependent children had much lower incomes and also depended more on social security benefits than on any other source of income. Those in lone parent with dependent children families received 44 per cent of their income in the form of means-tested benefits; these include income support and other benefits designed to supplement low incomes. On the other hand, retired couples obtained a similar proportion of their income from non-means-tested benefits, such as the state retirement pension.

Table 2.11 uses the HBAI analyses of the Family Expenditure Survey to show where people in each type of family fall within overall income distribution. If people in each type of family were dispersed equally throughout the income distribution, then 20 per cent of people in each family type would be in each quintile group. Lone parents and their dependent children are over represented in the lower part of the income distribution; in the period 1993-94 to 1994-95 just over three quarters were in the lowest two quintile groups. On the other hand, those in non-retired couples with dependent children are relatively evenly distributed between the groups while non-retired couples without dependent children are over represented at the top of the income distribution; 63 per cent of adults in these families were in the highest two of the five income groupings.

The income distribution can also be analysed by looking at the proportions of people whose equivalised income lies below various fractions of average (mean) income.

When assessing changes over time, it is important to realise that changes in the overall distribution have influenced the average income. The rapid growth in incomes further up the distribution has pulled up the value of average income. The proportion of the population below average income in 1979 was 59 per cent while the proportion below 1993-94 average income was 63 per cent (before housing costs).

HBAI analyses assign the same equivalised income to each member of the household including children. Consequently the position of children in the income distribution is a reflection of the income of the household in which they live. The proportion of dependent children in the United Kingdom with 'incomes' below half of the average is shown in Table 2.12. The proportion of dependent children with 'incomes' below half contemporary average income increased during the 1980s but has levelled in the 1990s. These trends are features of the widening income distribution in the 1980s influenced by increases in unemployment and in the number of lone parents. Once again, income differences can be seen between different family types. In the period 1993-94 to 1994-95 the proportion of dependent children living in lone parent families below half average income was double the proportion living in non-retired couple families.

Income levels, like families themselves, are not static and continually change over time. In fact people and households change positions in the income distribution all the time. Sometimes income mobility is associated with family changes. Such changes will affect equivalised income due to the changing demands on the resources of the household. The British Household Panel Survey (BHPS), which has been re-interviewing the same sample of people annually since 1991, has been used in Table 2.13 to examine year-on-year changes in the income and family circumstances of adults in Great Britain for the period 1991 to 1995.

### Percentage of dependent children who live in families with income[1] below half contemporary mean income[1]: by family type

| United Kingdom | | | Percentages |
| --- | --- | --- | --- |
| | 1981 | 1990-91 | 1993-1995[2] |
| Non-retired couples | 12 | 21 | 21 |
| Lone parents | 13 | 52 | 43 |
| All families | 12 | 26 | 25 |

1 Before housing costs.
2 Combined years: 1993-94 and 1994-95.
**Source: Department of Social Security from Family Expenditure Survey**

## 2.13

### Adults moving within the income distribution[1] between consecutive years: by type of family change, 1991 to 1995[2]

| Great Britain | | | Percentages |
| --- | --- | --- | --- |
| | Income fell 2 or more deciles | Income stable[3] | Income rose 2 or more deciles |
| No change | 12 | 75 | 13 |
| Birth only | 22 | 69 | 9 |
| Adult child departs only | 18 | 64 | 18 |
| Death of partner only | 13 | 59 | 29 |
| Child leaving parental home[4] | 52 | 30 | 18 |
| Join with partner[5] | | | |
|   Males | 26 | 50 | 24 |
|   Females | 17 | 49 | 34 |
| Separate from partner[6] | | | |
|   Males | 19 | 52 | 30 |
|   Females | 47 | 39 | 14 |
| Other changes | 15 | 58 | 27 |
| All adults | 14 | 72 | 14 |

1 Equivalised gross household income has been used to rank the adults.
2 Changes in income and household composition for the periods 1991 to 1992, 1992 to 1993, 1993 to 1994 and 1994 to 1995 have been analysed separately and then combined.
3 Income group did not change, or fell by one decile or increased by one decile.
4 The income change experienced by the departing child. Includes all children leaving their parental home except those who join with a partner in the same year.
5 Includes all those joining a partner regardless of other changes in the same year.
6 Includes all those who separate from a partner except those who had joined a partner in the same year.
**Source: British Household Panel Survey, ESRC Research Centre on Micro-social Change**

# 2.14

## Relative earnings[1] of male and female partners[2], 1995-96

| Great Britain | Percentages |
|---|---|
| | 1995-96 |
| Male earns over £100 more | 56 |
| Male earns £50-£100 more | 12 |
| Earnings are equal[3] | 19 |
| Female earns £50-£100 more | 5 |
| Female earns over £100 more | 9 |
| All couples[2] | 100 |

1 Gross weekly earnings from employment or self-employment.
2 Couples where both partners work full time.
3 Equal to within £50 per week.

**Source: Family Resources Survey, Department of Social Security**

Between 1991 and 1995, 13 per cent of adults in households, on average, experienced some type of family change each year. Of these changes, the birth of a child is more likely to result in a fall in equivalised income than a rise. This is because increases in household size cause a decrease in equivalised income and also, in some households, the mother may have left employment at least temporarily. Children leaving the parental home are likely to experience a fall in their household income: the equivalised income of the new household was two or more deciles lower in half of these cases. Almost half of women separating from their partners experienced a substantial drop in income, while men were more likely to experience a rise than a fall in these circumstances. This is because men are the main earners in the majority of partnerships, even where both partners work full time.

Table 2.14 compares the earnings of male and female partners who were both working full time in 1995-96 in Great Britain. The man earned at least £50 a week more than the woman in 68 per cent of these couples and in most of these cases the man earned over £100 a week more than the woman. In contrast, just 14 per cent of women earned at least £50 more than the man. The situation is even more unbalanced if a couple has dependent children: men earned at least £50 a week more than women in 74 per cent of these couples in 1995-96 while in just 12 per cent of cases the woman was earning at least £50 more than the man.

Where the head of the family is unemployed, or in low paid work, social security benefit payments are a major source of income. Overall, social security benefit expenditure on families was £17 billion in 1995-96 which was a rise of about three quarters in real terms on the level in 1981-82. It should be noted that this figure does not include expenditure on income support and housing benefit (Social Fund) claimants except in the case of lone parents.

# 2.15

## Recipients of benefits for families

| Great Britain | | | | | Thousands |
|---|---|---|---|---|---|
| | 1981-82 | 1986-87 | 1991-92 | 1994-95 | 1995-96 |
| **Child benefit** | | | | | |
| Number of dependent children | 13,079 | 12,217 | 12,401 | 12,730 | 12,790 |
| Number of families | 7,174 | 6,816 | 6,852 | 7,000 | 7,038 |
| **Lone parent families** | | | | | |
| One parent benefit only | 323 | 354 | 475 | 576 | 614 |
| One parent benefit and income support | 146 | 253 | 361 | 373 | 388 |
| Income support only | 222 | 376 | 584 | 676 | 672 |
| **Other benefits** | | | | | |
| Maternity allowance | 115 | 109 | 11 | 9 | .. |
| Statutory maternity pay | . | . | 85 | 95 | .. |
| Family credit | 139 | 218 | 356 | 602 | 667 |

**Source: Department of Social Security**

Table 2.15 shows the rapid increase in the number of lone parent families receiving certain benefits over this period. One parent benefit or income support, or both benefits together, were received by more than twice as many lone parent families in 1995-96 as in 1981-82. This reflects to a great extent the increase in the number of lone parent families.

Families receive a wide range of benefits. Around three quarters of families in Great Britain received some sort of social security benefit in 1995-96 (Table 2.16). Families comprising non-retired couples with no dependent children were less likely to receive most benefits than any other family type and just three out of ten of these families received any type of benefit at all. In contrast, virtually all families with dependent children and retired couples received at least one type of benefit. Most retired couples received the state retirement pension while nearly all non-retired couple and lone parent with dependent children families received child benefit. In 1995-96, over 7 million of these families in Great Britain received child benefit.

Non-retired couples with dependent children were much less likely than lone parents with dependent children to receive any other benefits, and those which they did receive were mostly income-related (Chart 2.17). Lone parent with dependent children families were very likely to receive income-related benefits such as income support. Interestingly, the proportions of non-retired couple and lone parent benefit units who received income-related benefits both increased with the number of dependent children in the benefit unit.

Benefits, however, are not the only means of financial assistance to families with children. The *Child Support Act 1991* introduced a new system intended to remove discretion from the assessment of child maintenance after marriage break up and ensure that both parents meet their responsibilities towards the support of their children. In April 1993 the Child Support Agency (CSA) was set up to replace the role of the courts in assessing, collecting and enforcing child maintenance. During 1995-96 the CSA dealt with over 300 thousand cases. Although this was actually a fall in the number of cases compared with the previous year, the amount of maintenance collected more than doubled. This was due to a larger amount of resources being concentrated on managing the maintenance accounts for existing clients.

### Percentage of families receiving benefits, 1995-96

**Great Britain**                                                                           Percentages

|  | Child benefit | Retire-ment pension | Council tax benefit | Housing benefit | Income support | Unemp-loyment benefit | Any benefit |
|---|---|---|---|---|---|---|---|
| Retired couples | 1 | 96 | 22 | 14 | 7 | - | 100 |
| Non-retired couples |  |  |  |  |  |  |  |
|   Dependent children | 98 | - | 12 | 10 | 10 | 2 | 99 |
|   No dependent children | - | 7 | 8 | 5 | 6 | 2 | 30 |
| Lone parents |  |  |  |  |  |  |  |
|   Dependent children | 98 | 0 | 62 | 60 | 63 | - | 99 |
| All families | 48 | 19 | 18 | 15 | 14 | 1 | 75 |

*Source: Family Resources Survey, Department of Social Security*

### Percentage of families with dependent children receiving selected benefits, 1995-96

**Great Britain**

Percentages

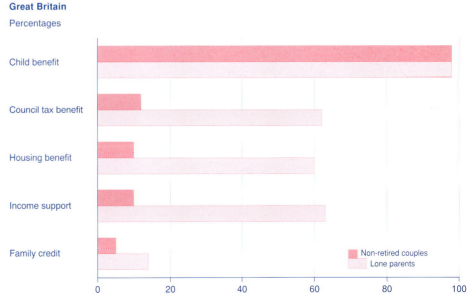

*Source: Family Resources Survey, Department of Social Security*

# 2.18

## Net weekly spending power[1]: by gross weekly earnings[2] and family type, April 1996

**Great Britain**

£ per week

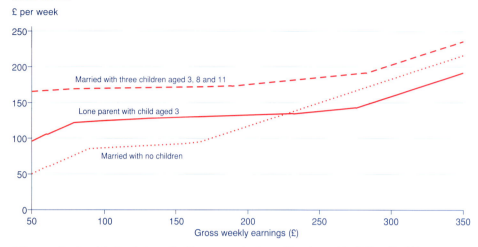

Married with three children aged 3, 8 and 11

Lone parent with child aged 3

Married with no children

Gross weekly earnings (£)

1 Gross earnings less deductions for tax, national insurance, rent and council tax, plus receipts of all benefits which are applicable for a family paying average local authority rent. A deduction of £40 for childcare costs has been made in the case of the lone parent family only.
2 Gross earnings from full-time work where head of household only is in employment.

**Source: Department of Social Security**

# 2.19

## Savings: by family type, 1995-96

**Great Britain**

Percentages

| | No savings | Less than £3,000 | £3,000 but less than £10,000 | £10,000 but less than £20,000 | £20,000 or more | All |
|---|---|---|---|---|---|---|
| Retired couples | 20 | 21 | 16 | 12 | 31 | 100 |
| Non-retired couples | | | | | | |
| Dependent children | 33 | 34 | 18 | 7 | 8 | 100 |
| No dependent children | 22 | 29 | 21 | 10 | 18 | 100 |
| Lone parents | | | | | | |
| Dependent children | 73 | 22 | 3 | 1 | 1 | 100 |
| All families | 32 | 28 | 17 | 8 | 15 | 100 |

**Source: Family Resources Survey, Department of Social Security**

Entitlement to different benefits changes as earnings change. At one time it was possible for an increase in earnings to cause a fall in net income because of the withdrawal of benefits; this was known as the poverty trap. The effect of the poverty trap has been lessened by social security reforms and, in general, net income increases with gross income. Despite this Chart 2.18, which models changes in weekly spending power by level of earnings, is fairly flat in places showing that, in some ranges of income, spending power increases only very slowly. Changes in earnings may not lead immediately to changes in benefit entitlement, as family credit is paid at the same rate for six months before being reassessed.

At gross earnings of £50 per week in April 1996 the spending power of the three family types varied considerably. The married couple with no children paid no deductions and received maximum housing benefit and council tax benefit, leaving them with a net income of £50. The married couple with three children aged 3,8 and 11 could also claim family credit and child benefit and received a net income of £165. The difference narrowed as earnings increased and income-related benefits tapered off, until at earnings of just over £280 a week the three child family lost entitlement to family credit. Their spending power was then about £20 more than the couple with no children; this was made up of child benefit partly offset by higher rents and council tax.

The model used for the chart takes net income, or weekly spending power after tax, where national insurance contributions, rent and council tax payments have been deducted and receipts of benefits added. In order to model net income, it is assumed that there is no income other than the earnings of the head of household, who is in full-time employment, and social security benefits, for which full entitlement is claimed; they have only their personal tax allowances; they live in local authority rented accommodation; they are not contracted out of the state pension scheme; and the lone parent family incur childcare costs of £40 per week.

The amount of income available to a household has an obvious effect on the amount of savings a household can accumulate. The FRS collects information about the types, and amounts, of savings people have. However, response to these types of questions is relatively low and some estimation is involved, so bands of savings have been used.

Lone parents with dependent children, who have a low proportion of their income derived from earnings, are the most likely not to have any savings at all; almost three quarters of these families in Great Britain did not have any savings in 1995-96 (Table 2.19). In contrast, almost a third of retired couples had savings of more than £20 thousand.

The lower level of savings in some family types is also reflected in the way they hold their savings. Current accounts were the most common type of account although only 54 per cent of lone parents with dependent children held one of these. In comparison, 90 per cent of non-retired couples with dependent children held a current account. They also quite often had other types of accounts: 65 per cent of non-retired couples with dependent children had a building society account, 32 per cent held premium bonds and 21 per cent held stocks and shares.

**Household expenditure: by family type[1], 1995-96**

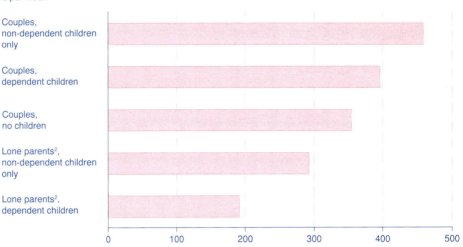

**United Kingdom**

£ per week

1 Excludes retired families.
2 Excludes lone parent families living with other families.
**Source: Family Expenditure Survey, Office for National Statistics**

## Expenditure

The average expenditure of different types of family is, of course, closely related to their income. The Family Expenditure Survey (FES) is the major source of information on the expenditure of families and results from the 1995-96 survey in the United Kingdom are used in this section. All the analyses adopt the standard definitions of different family types that have been used as much as possible in this report. However, in this section, retired families have been excluded from the analyses as they have very different expenditure habits to families headed by younger people.

Families with only non-dependent children spend more, on average, than those with dependent children because they tend to have higher incomes. As might be expected, lone parents with dependent children had the lowest level of expenditure at just over £190 per week on average in 1995-96 (Chart 2.20). In contrast, couples with only non-dependent children spent nearly two and half times this amount per week.

# 2.21

## Household expenditure: by family type[1] and type of expenditure, 1995-96

United Kingdom                                                                                    Percentages

| | Couples | | | Lone parents[2] | |
| | Dependent children | Non-dependent children only | No children | Dependent children | Non-dependent children only |
|---|---|---|---|---|---|
| Food | 19 | 18 | 16 | 22 | 18 |
| Housing | 18 | 11 | 17 | 14 | 13 |
| Leisure goods and services | 15 | 17 | 17 | 13 | 15 |
| Household goods and services | 13 | 12 | 14 | 14 | 11 |
| Motoring | 12 | 17 | 14 | 9 | 12 |
| Clothing and footwear | 6 | 7 | 6 | 8 | 7 |
| | | | | | |
| Fuel, light and power | 4 | 4 | 4 | 7 | 5 |
| Personal goods and services | 4 | 4 | 4 | 4 | 4 |
| Alcohol | 3 | 6 | 4 | 2 | 6 |
| Fares and other travel costs | 2 | 2 | 2 | 3 | 5 |
| Tobacco | 2 | 2 | 2 | 3 | 3 |
| Other goods and services | 1 | - | - | 2 | - |
| | | | | | |
| All household expenditure[3] | | | | | |
| (=100%)(£ per week) | 396.50 | 459.10 | 355.00 | 192.40 | 293.40 |

1 Excludes retired families.
2 Excludes lone parent families living with other families.
3 Expenditure rounded to nearest ten pence.

**Source: Family Expenditure Survey, Office for National Statistics**

# 2.22

## Household expenditure[1] on selected items: by family type[2], 1995-96

United Kingdom                                                                                    £ per week

| | Couples | | | Lone parents[3] | |
| | Dependent children | Non-dependent children only | No children | Dependent children | Non-dependent children only |
|---|---|---|---|---|---|
| Restaurant meals | 8.80 | 13.10 | 10.50 | 3.50 | 6.70 |
| Take away meals | 3.20 | 3.70 | 2.20 | 1.80 | 2.50 |
| Confectionery | 0.80 | 0.90 | 0.40 | 0.40 | 0.70 |
| Ice cream | 0.40 | 0.30 | 0.20 | 0.30 | 0.20 |
| | | | | | |
| Hotel and holiday abroad | 8.40 | 13.60 | 12.50 | 3.00 | 4.80 |
| National Lottery and scratchcards | 2.80 | 4.50 | 2.90 | 1.50 | 3.00 |
| Newspapers | 2.00 | 3.30 | 2.40 | 0.90 | 2.40 |
| Cinema and theatre | 1.20 | 1.70 | 1.00 | 0.60 | 0.70 |

1 Expenditure rounded to nearest ten pence.
2 Excludes retired families.
3 Excludes lone parent families living with other families.

**Source: Family Expenditure Survey, Office for National Statistics**

All families with children spend a greater proportion of their expenditure on food than any other of the main expenditure categories shown in Table 2.21. Again, lone parents with dependent children stand out as having distinctly different spending patterns compared with other types of families. A greater proportion of their expenditure went on food, and on some of the other essentials such as fuel, light and power than was the case for other families. They did however spend a smaller proportion than couple families with dependent children on housing - reflecting their tendency to live in social sector rented accommodation (see Table 2.26). A smaller proportion of lone parent with dependent children families' expenditure also went on motoring than was the case for couple families with dependent children. This can be explained by the fact that they are less likely to have a car (see Table 3.6).

Table 2.22 shows that lone parents with dependent children spend much less than other families on these items that are sometimes thought of as luxuries. However, it should be noted that there are, on average, fewer people in lone parent families. Lone parents with dependent children spend an average of £3.50 a week on restaurant meals whereas couples with dependent children spend £8.80 on this type of expenditure. The difference in expenditure on ice cream for these two types of family is not so great. Lone parents with dependent children spend an average of about 30 pence a week while couples with dependent children spend roughly 40 pence a week. A small part of this difference can be explained by the fact that the average number of children in lone parent families is slightly smaller than in couple families.

# 2.23

Lone parents gave their dependent children slightly less pocket money on average than married couples (Table 2.23). Cohabiting couples appear to be most frugal with their money in this respect giving each of their dependent children less than £1 per week on average. However, this may be due to the fact that they are more likely to have younger children than other families (see Table 1.27). A married couple with one dependent child gave, on average, more than three times the amount of pocket money as a cohabiting couple with one dependent child. The average amount of pocket money given to a dependent child was about £1.80 per week.

Information about children's spending was obtained through the FES for the first time in 1995-96. Children aged 7 to 15 used diaries to record their spending over a two week period. Some preliminary results are given in Chart 2.24 and Table 2.25.

Children's expenditure in the United Kingdom in 1995-96 was, on average, £8.40 per week and, as might be expected, it increased with age. Boys and girls aged seven to eight spent, on average, just over £4 and £3 per week respectively while both boys and girls aged 15 spent almost £17 per week (Chart 2.24). Younger boys tend to spend slightly more, on average, than younger girls, while older girls spend more than boys of the same age. In particular, teenage girls aged 13 to 14 spend £2 more a week than boys of the same age.

As Table 2.23 showed, dependent children receive £1.80 a week in pocket money. The amount of pocket money received by children also increases with age, with the amount given to children under seven being small. For those children aged between 7 and 15 pocket money on average is £3.10 per week. However, children's spending is not funded by pocket money alone. They also receive money from a variety of other sources, including money they earned themselves and cash gifts from parents or other relatives. In addition, a further source of income for children is that given to them by parents for school dinners and fares to and from school. The expenditure on these items is included in the children's spending figures.

**Pocket money[1] given to dependent children: by family type[2], 1995-96**

| United Kingdom | £ per week per child |
|---|---|
| | 1995-96 |
| **Married couples** | |
| One dependent child | 2.20 |
| Two dependent children | 1.80 |
| **Cohabiting couples** | |
| One dependent child | 0.70 |
| Two dependent children | 0.90 |
| **Lone parents[3]** | |
| One dependent child | 2.00 |
| Two dependent children | 1.50 |
| **All families with dependent children** | 1.80 |

1 Money given rounded to nearest ten pence.
2 Excludes retired families.
3 Excludes lone parent families living with other families.
*Source: Family Expenditure Survey, Office for National Statistics*

# 2.24

**Children's expenditure: by age and gender, 1995-96**

**United Kingdom**
£ per week

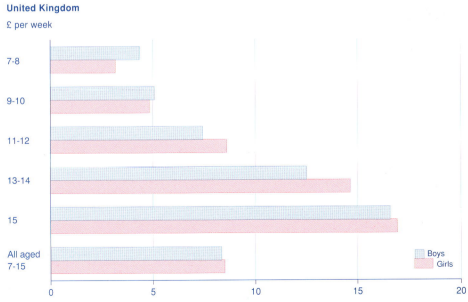

*Source: Family Expenditure Survey, Office for National Statistics*

# 2.25

## Children's expenditure: by age and type of expenditure, 1995-96

United Kingdom — Percentages

| | Food | Leisure goods | Leisure services | House-hold goods | Clothing and footwear | Fares[1] | Other | Average expenditure (=100%) (£ per week[2]) |
|---|---|---|---|---|---|---|---|---|
| 7-8 | 41 | 29 | 10 | 7 | 4 | 1 | 8 | 3.80 |
| 9-10 | 41 | 30 | 9 | 8 | 4 | 2 | 6 | 5.00 |
| 11-12 | 43 | 15 | 10 | 8 | 9 | 5 | 9 | 8.00 |
| 13-14 | 34 | 17 | 10 | 6 | 19 | 6 | 10 | 13.50 |
| 15 | 35 | 14 | 9 | 4 | 17 | 7 | 12 | 16.80 |
| All aged 7-15 | 38 | 19 | 10 | 6 | 13 | 5 | 9 | 8.40 |

1 Includes other travel costs.
2 Expenditure rounded to nearest ten pence.

*Source: Family Expenditure Survey, Office for National Statistics*

The proportion of children's expenditure that is spent on various items also varies with their age (Table 2.25). Children aged under 11 generally spent a greater proportion of their money on food and leisure goods than those aged 11 to 15. In particular, these younger children spent a high proportion of their money on toys, books and sweets. However, children aged 11 to 15, and especially teenagers, spent a greater proportion of their money on clothing than younger children. Additionally, the proportion of children's expenditure on fares increased for each age group as older children are more likely to travel by themselves on school journeys and so pay for their own ticket, and also possibly because older children have more freedom to go out and about by themselves than younger children.

# 2.26

## Housing tenure: by family type, 1995-96

United Kingdom — Percentages

| | Owned outright | Owned with mortgage | Rented from social sector | Rented privately | All tenures |
|---|---|---|---|---|---|
| **Married couples** | | | | | |
| Dependent children | 7 | 72 | 13 | 7 | 100 |
| Non-dependent children only | 30 | 54 | 12 | 4 | 100 |
| No children | 43 | 37 | 14 | 6 | 100 |
| All married couples | 27 | 54 | 13 | 6 | 100 |
| **Cohabiting couples** | | | | | |
| Dependent children | - | 55 | 36 | 10 | 100 |
| Non-dependent children only | 21 | 69 | 10 | - | 100 |
| No children | 8 | 63 | 10 | 18 | 100 |
| All cohabiting couples | 6 | 60 | 19 | 15 | 100 |
| **Lone parents** | | | | | |
| Dependent children | 7 | 30 | 52 | 10 | 100 |
| Non-dependent children only | 35 | 27 | 31 | 8 | 100 |
| All lone parents | 15 | 29 | 46 | 10 | 100 |
| **All families** | 23 | 51 | 18 | 7 | 100 |

*Source: General Household Survey, Office for National Statistics; Continuous Household Survey, Northern Ireland Statistics and Research Agency*

## Homes

The home that a family lives in is an important part of the lives of its members. The amount of money that is spent on accommodation, in most cases, forms one of the largest proportions of a family's expenditure, whether they are renting the accommodation or own it with a mortgage. The financial position of the family will often determine the type, standard and location of their home, and these factors can have an impact on the quality of life experienced by family members. Indeed, some characteristics of housing are used as key indicators of standards of living.

Housing tenure has traditionally been closely related to the economic status, social class and age of the occupiers and therefore tenure varies considerably for different types of family. In general, married couple families are much more likely to own their property either outright or with a mortgage than other families, while lone parent families are much more likely to be renting (Table 2.26). This pattern is particularly marked for families with dependent children; four fifths of married couples with dependent children were owner-occupiers in 1995-96, whereas just over three fifths of lone parents with dependent children were renting. The majority of these lone parent families were renting from the social sector, that is from a local authority or housing association.

The balance between married couples who own their home outright and those with a mortgage is very different according to whether or not they have dependent children. Seven out of ten married couples with dependent children owned their home with a mortgage compared with just over half of those with non-dependent children and less than two fifths of those with no children. This is due to the lifecycle effect - adults without dependent children are on average older than other types of families and therefore will usually have had more time to pay off their mortgages. Indeed, seven out of ten heads of households who were outright owner-occupiers were over 60 in 1995-96.

Some types of families are more likely to live in certain types of dwellings than others. In 1995-96, 29 per cent of couple families lived in detached houses compared with 9 per cent of lone parent families (Table 2.27). Lone parent families were most likely to live

in terraced houses with 39 per cent of them living in this type of dwelling. They were also twice as likely as couple families to be living in purpose-built flats or maisonettes. Terraced houses, flats and maisonettes are generally cheaper to buy or rent than detached and semi-detached houses. Therefore it is not surprising that a greater proportion of lone parent families live in these dwellings than other families. However, part of the reason why these sorts of dwellings are often cheaper is that they are also usually smaller than detached or semi-detached houses. Consequently lone parents tend to be more likely to be living in overcrowded and poorer quality accommodation than other families.

### Type of dwelling: by family type, 1995-96

**United Kingdom** — Percentages

| | House or bungalow | | | Flat or maisonette | | | |
|---|---|---|---|---|---|---|---|
| | Detached | Semi-detached | Terraced | Purpose-built | Con-verted | Other dwellings | All dwellings |
| **Couples** | | | | | | | |
| Dependent children | 28 | 37 | 29 | 5 | 1 | - | 100 |
| Non-dependent children only | 29 | 42 | 24 | 3 | - | 1 | 100 |
| No children | 29 | 32 | 25 | 10 | 3 | 1 | 100 |
| All couples | 29 | 35 | 26 | 7 | 2 | 1 | 100 |
| **Lone parent families** | | | | | | | |
| Dependent children | 7 | 32 | 40 | 18 | 2 | - | 100 |
| Non-dependent children only | 15 | 35 | 36 | 12 | 2 | 1 | 100 |
| All lone parents | 9 | 33 | 39 | 16 | 2 | - | 100 |
| **All families** | 26 | 35 | 28 | 9 | 2 | 1 | 100 |

*Source: General Household Survey, Office for National Statistics; Continuous Household Survey, Northern Ireland Statistics and Research Agency*

# 2.28

## Under-occupation[1] and overcrowding[2]: by family type, 1995-96

**United Kingdom**

Percentages

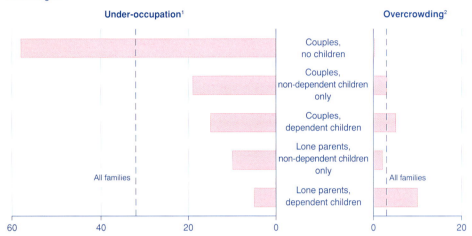

1 Percentage of families in each family type who were living in accommodation which was two or more above bedroom standard.
2 Percentage of families in each family type who were living in accommodation which was one or more below bedroom standard.
**Source: General Household Survey, Office for National Statistics; Continuous Household Survey, Northern Ireland Statistics and Research Agency**

# 2.29

## Percentage of families with central heating, 1995-96

| United Kingdom | Percentages |
|---|---|
| | 1995-96 |
| **Married couples** | |
| Dependent children | 92 |
| No dependent children[1] | 89 |
| **Cohabiting couples** | |
| Dependent children | 87 |
| No dependent children[1] | 87 |
| **Lone parents** | |
| Dependent children | 84 |
| Non-dependent children only | 80 |
| **All families** | 89 |

1 Comprises families with non-dependent children only and those with no children.
**Source: General Household Survey, Office for National Statistics; Continuous Household Survey, Northern Ireland Statistics and Research Agency**

One measure of overcrowding is the bedroom standard which sets a standard for the number of bedrooms a household needs depending on its composition and the relationship of its members to each other. This standard is then compared with the actual number of bedrooms available to the household. Where the number of rooms is one or more below the bedroom standard, households are classified as overcrowded, whereas if the number of rooms is two or more above the bedroom standard they are treated as under-occupied.

Chart 2.28 uses these differences from the bedroom standard to show the proportion of each type of family in the United Kingdom who lived in overcrowded and under-occupied accommodation in 1995-96. In general, families with dependent children are more likely than those without dependent children to live in

accommodation below the bedroom standard. In addition, lone parents with dependent children are twice as likely as couples with dependent children to live in accommodation that is classified as overcrowded: one in ten of these families were in this situation in 1995-96. In contrast, couples with no children often occupy accommodation well above the standard; almost six in ten of these families lived in homes that were considered to be under-occupied.

In the past, whether or not accommodation was equipped with basic amenities was a widely used method of assessing housing standards. Nowadays very few family homes lack basic amenities; for example, less than 1 per cent of households lack facilities such as a bath/shower or an internal flush toilet. Because of this, whether a home has central heating or not is now a better indicator of a family's standard of housing. In 1995-96, almost nine out of ten families lived in accommodation with central heating in the United Kingdom (Table 2.29). Although there was little variation between the different family types, a lower proportion of lone parent families than other families had central heating in their homes. In addition, married couple families were slightly more likely than cohabiting couple families to have central heating.

As well as the number of rooms and facilities in the accommodation, other factors such as the location, state of repair, layout, size of rooms and general appearance will also affect whether or not families are satisfied overall with their housing. About nine out of ten families in England were very, or fairly, satisfied overall with their accommodation in 1995-96. However, it needs to be borne in mind that people do tend to make positive responses when faced with generalised questions about satisfaction.

Overall satisfaction with accommodation is linked to the type of accommodation in which families live. Those who rent and those who live in flats are more likely to be dissatisfied with their accommodation than those who own their accommodation and those who live in detached or semi-detached houses. As might be expected, lone parents with dependent children, who are more commonly found in rented accommodation and flats, were twice as likely to be dissatisfied with their housing as any other type of family (Chart 2.30); 16 per cent of lone parents with dependent children were dissatisfied with their accommodation overall. The most common concern families had about their housing was insulation and draught-proofing with one in five families being slightly, or very, dissatisfied with this aspect of their accommodation. State of repair and heating were the next most commonly cited concerns, but only around 15 per cent of families said they were dissatisfied with their housing in these two respects.

Results from the 1995-96 Survey of English Housing also revealed that although most households got on with their neighbours, a greater proportion of lone parents with dependent children than other households reported that they had experienced problems with neighbours. This is not surprising as, since they are more

**Dissatisfaction[1] with housing: by family type, 1995-96**

**England**
Percentages

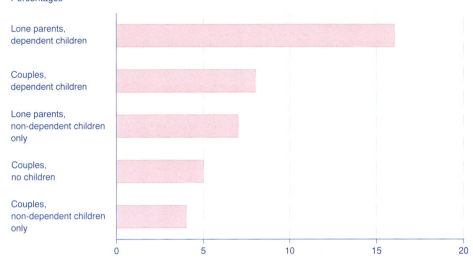

1 Percentage of households who said that they were either 'slightly dissatisfied' or 'very dissatisfied' with their housing.
**Source: Survey of English Housing, Department of the Environment, Transport and the Regions**

commonly found in flats (and therefore often live close to other households), they are more likely to live in deprived areas than other families. Noise was the most common problem - over a quarter of lone parents with dependent children said that this was a problem or serious problem. Just over one in five lone parents with dependent children also mentioned that cars and children out of control had been problems.

When families are dissatisfied with their housing one solution may be to move. The most common reason for moving in 1995-96 was people wanting larger or better accommodation: 22 per cent of all moves resulted from this desire. However, many moves are for reasons that are specifically family-related and about one in twelve of all moves were made because of divorce or separation.

# 2.31

## Tenure one year after divorce[1]: by gender and tenure of former matrimonial home, 1991-1994[2]

**Great Britain**                                                                                    Percentages

| | Tenure of former matrimonial home | | | |
| --- | --- | --- | --- | --- |
| | Owner-occupied | Rented from social sector | Rented privately | All tenures |
| **Tenure one year after divorce** | | | | |
| Males | | | | |
| Owned outright | 6 | 0 | 0 | 4 |
| Owned with mortgage | 55 | 5 | 17 | 37 |
| Rented from social sector | 3 | 47 | 16 | 17 |
| Rented privately | 11 | 12 | 47 | 15 |
| Not a householder | 25 | 35 | 21 | 27 |
| | | | | |
| All males | 100 | 100 | 100 | 100 |
| | | | | |
| Females | | | | |
| Owned outright | 10 | - | 2 | 6 |
| Owned with mortgage | 57 | 3 | 14 | 37 |
| Rented from social sector | 11 | 82 | 18 | 33 |
| Rented privately | 5 | 3 | 33 | 7 |
| Not a householder | 18 | 11 | 33 | 17 |
| | | | | |
| All females | 100 | 100 | 100 | 100 |

1 Divorces in 1980 or later where the person had not remarried by the time of interview.
2 Combined years: 1991-92, 1992-93 and 1993-94.
**Source: General Household Survey, Office for National Statistics**

In the period 1991-92 to 1993-94 the General Household Survey interviewed people who had divorced in 1980 or later, and had not remarried by the time they were interviewed. The effects of divorce on the tenure of these people are examined in Table 2.31 which compares the tenure of their former matrimonial home with their tenure one year after divorce.

An obvious consequence of divorce is that one household may be replaced by two, one or both of which may change tenure. Many couples require two incomes in order to buy housing and on separation one person may not have the financial resources to purchase a home by themselves. Indeed, two fifths of men and a third of women who had lived as owner-occupiers before divorce no longer did so one year after divorcing. In addition, some divorcees may cease to be householders in their own right by moving into someone else's household or back to their parents' home. The majority of people, however, who had divorced and had not remarried, had not changed tenure one year after their divorce. The proportion of women who had not changed tenure was particularly high among those renting social sector housing - four out of five of these women had not changed tenure. Men were more likely than women to have changed tenure following divorce. This is not unexpected as women were more likely to be living in the former matrimonial home one year after divorce: 43 per cent were doing so compared with 30 per cent of men.

Some types of families are more prone to experiencing difficulties paying their rent or mortgage than others. Rent arrears were most likely to be a problem for families with dependent children: just over one in eight of these families in England were behind with their payments in 1995-96 (Chart 2.32). Lone parents with dependent children were the most likely to be in arrears with their mortgage payments; they were four times as likely as couples with dependent children to be in this position.

Part III of the Housing Act 1985 and its Scottish equivalent require local authorities to help homeless people in defined categories of 'priority need'. Court orders resulting from mortgage default or rent arrears were the reasons why a tenth of homeless people in England, Wales and Northern Ireland were found accommodation by local authorities in 1994. More common reasons were that people's parents, relatives or friends were no longer able or willing to provide accommodation for them or that a relationship with a partner had broken down.

Figures relating to the United Kingdom show that the largest category of the homeless people found accommodation in 1994 were families with young children, making up three fifths of the total. The second largest category, accounting for an eighth of the total, was households where one of the members was pregnant.

The 1995-96 Survey of English Housing asked people if they had experienced homelessness within the last ten years. Reporting of homelessness was particularly high among lone parent with dependent children households. Around three in ten people from these households considered themselves to have been homeless in the last ten years. This was more than four times the proportion for couples with dependent children. Given this fact, it is perhaps not surprising that a higher proportion of lone parents reported that they lived in less expensive and lower quality accommodation than those in other types of families.

**Families with mortgage[1] and rent[2] arrears, 1995-96**

**England**

Percentages

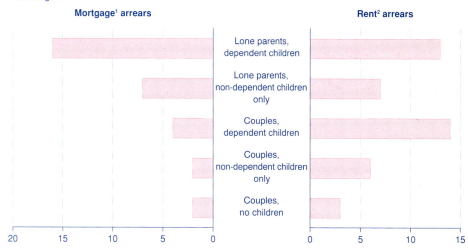

1 Percentage of households with a mortgage in each household type, who were in arrears.
2 Percentage of households who were renting in each household type, who were in arrears.
**Source: Survey of English Housing, Department of the Environment, Transport and the Regions**

# 3

# Family life

## Lifestyles

The debate on the state of the modern family has centred on the shift away from traditional family values. Whereas Chapter One focuses on the way families are composed and how this has changed in recent years, this chapter aims to give a more comprehensive picture of how family members spend their time together and how they relate to each other. It also illustrates what it means to be a family, the enduring importance of families in people's lives and the often complex relationships that exist within the family unit.

How people spend their time is related to family composition and other factors such as employment status, age and gender. In May 1995 the Omnibus Survey asked people in Great Britain about the main activities they spent their time on throughout the day. Owing to the small sample size, the results shown in the following two tables should be interpreted with caution. It is also important to bear in mind that only one 'main' activity could be reported at any one time. For example, if an individual was watching television while looking after a child, then they recorded only the activity which they considered to be the primary activity.

# Lifestyles

## 3.1

### Time use of adults[1]: by family type, May 1995

**Great Britain** Hours and minutes per day

| | Couples | | Lone parents |
| --- | --- | --- | --- |
| | Dependent children | No dependent children | Dependent children |
| Sleep | 8:19 | 8:42 | 8:41 |
| Cooking, routine housework | 1:36 | 1:28 | 2:21 |
| Personal care | 0:38 | 0:47 | 0:41 |
| Care of children and adults | 1:06 | 0:05 | 1:34 |
| TV and radio | 2:09 | 2:36 | 2:23 |
| Gardening and DIY | 0:30 | 0:50 | 0:35 |
| Other home leisure[2] | 0:49 | 1:15 | 1:03 |
| | | | |
| Eating at home | 0:57 | 1:06 | 0:54 |
| Paid work | 3:29 | 3:14 | 1:48 |
| Socialising[3] | 0:57 | 1:04 | 1:06 |
| Shopping | 0:32 | 0:38 | 0:36 |
| Eating or drinking out | 0:29 | 0:29 | 0:15 |
| Travel | 0:56 | 0:45 | 0:34 |
| Other out-of-home leisure[4] | 1:23 | 0:50 | 1:13 |

*1 Components do not add to 24 hours due to rounding.*
*2 Includes study at home.*
*3 Includes telephone conversations.*
*4 Includes education, voluntary work and various other leisure activities.*
***Source: Omnibus Survey, Office for National Statistics***

## 3.2

### Time use of parents[1]: by gender, May 1995

**Great Britain** Hours and minutes per day

| | Fathers | Mothers |
| --- | --- | --- |
| Sleep | 7:59 | 8:26 |
| Cooking, routine housework | 0:41 | 2:59 |
| Personal care | 0:36 | 0:42 |
| Care of children and adults | 0:54 | 1:56 |
| TV and radio | 2:24 | 2:04 |
| Gardening and DIY | 0:41 | 0:22 |
| Other home leisure[2] | 0:46 | 0:32 |
| | | |
| Eating at home | 0:52 | 1:00 |
| Paid work | 5:31 | 2:06 |
| Socialising[3] | 0:43 | 1:05 |
| Shopping | 0:24 | 0:46 |
| Eating or drinking out | 0:35 | 0:19 |
| Travel | 1:00 | 0:46 |
| Other out-of home leisure[4] | 0:48 | 0:46 |

*1 Parents living with dependent children aged under 16.*
*Components do not add to 24 hours due to rounding.*
*2 Includes study at home.*
*3 Includes telephone conversations.*
*4 Includes education, voluntary work and various other leisure activities.*
***Source: Omnibus Survey, Office for National Statistics***

Among families with dependent children, lone parents spend more time than couples on routine domestic activities such as housework, and also on childcare (Table 3.1). This, by definition, reflects the absence of a second parent in such families. When compared with couples with dependent children, this higher level of time spent on routine activities is offset by less time spent in paid work and travelling. On average, lone parents with dependent children spend less than two hours a day in paid work, compared with an average of three and a half hours for couples with dependent children. After work and sleep, watching television or listening to the radio is the next major activity for couple families, though there is very wide variation in the amount of time people spend on these activities.

Overall, couples without dependent children spend more time than those with such children on some leisure activities, such as watching television or listening to the radio, and less time caring for others. They also spend more time on a range of other personal and domestic activities.

There are also distinct differences in the time spent by mothers and fathers on different activities (Table 3.2). Fathers spend more time in paid work, which is unsurprising in the context of a labour market where fewer mothers are in employment and many work part time. On average, mothers spend around three hours a day primarily on housework and cooking, markedly more than fathers. Even those mothers in paid work continue to spend more time than fathers on such activities. Information on the economic activity status of mothers is contained in Chapter Two.

Mothers also spend about twice as long as fathers looking after children as a primary activity, though all parents spend more time looking after younger children than those of school age. While the amount of time spent on some activities varies considerably according to whether parents are in paid employment, gender differences in parents' time use appear to persist despite a variety of lifestyles in different families.

It does not appear that traditional gender roles have changed much, and indeed the prospect of this occurring in the next generation also seems unlikely. The Youth Lifestyles Survey (YLS) was carried out for the Home Office between November 1992 and January 1993. It found that while 32 per cent of young women aged between 14 and 25 in England and Wales usually, or always, did the household shopping, only 17 per cent of young men did likewise (Chart 3.3). Similar differences exist with other household tasks. Just under half of young men said that they never washed their own clothes, which compared with just over a quarter of young women who said that they never did so. Interestingly, the same survey also showed that while a quarter of young women usually, or always, looked after younger children in the household, only around one in ten young men did the same.

Having a child can obviously have far reaching implications for the parents, with virtually all aspects of their lifestyle affected in one way or another. The Value of a Mum survey, which was carried out for Legal and General in Great Britain in August 1996, attempted to measure some of these. The survey found that before starting their family, a third of parents with children aged 18 and under had felt unprepared for parenthood. One reason that was given was the amount of extra work involved.

Mothers and fathers felt differently about the impact of having children. For example, 20 per cent of fathers compared with 14 per cent of mothers felt that lack of money was the biggest difference that having children had made. Similarly, 11 per cent of fathers complained of having no social life after the birth of their children compared with 7 per cent of mothers who made the same claim.

**Young people who usually perform certain household tasks[1]: by gender, 1992-93[2]**

**England & Wales**
Percentages

1 People aged 14 to 25 who said that they usually or always did each of the listed household tasks.
2 November 1992 to January 1993.
**Source: Youth Lifestyles Survey, Home Office**

Table 3.4 demonstrates some of the possible effects of having children on social contacts. Even when social contact does take place it can often be dominated by child-related topics. Indeed, 58 per cent of mothers claimed that children were their main topic of conversation when they got together with their friends, while 38 per cent of fathers felt the same.

Half of the parents interviewed in the survey felt that they did not spend as much time as they would like together as a family and three quarters of those said that work was the main reason for this, particularly in the case of fathers. When questioned about the worst aspect of being a parent, one in five parents said that it was having no time alone, and one in eight said that it was having no time alone with their partner.

**3.4**

**Effect of having children on parents'[1] social contacts, August 1996**

| Great Britain | Percentages |
|---|---|
| | August 1996 |
| No change to circle of friends | 34 |
| Now socialise with people with children of the same age | 24 |
| Have a wider circle of friends | 21 |
| Lost contact with former friends who don't have children | 17 |
| Social circle has shrunk | 14 |
| Women making lasting friendships at maternity classes, National Childbirth Trust, etc | 10 |

1 Adults with children aged 18 and under. Respondents were allowed to give more than one answer.
**Source: Research Services Ltd for Legal & General Group plc**

# 3.5

## Families with consumer durables: by family type, 1995-96

United Kingdom      Percentages

| | Couples | | | Lone parents | |
|---|---|---|---|---|---|
| | Dependent children | Non-dependent children only | No children | Dependent children | Non-dependent children only |
| Colour television | 99 | 99 | 99 | 96 | 96 |
| Black and white television only | 1 | - | 1 | 3 | 2 |
| Washing machine | 99 | 98 | 96 | 96 | 91 |
| Deep freezer | 98 | 98 | 94 | 91 | 90 |
| Telephone | 96 | 98 | 97 | 83 | 92 |
| Video recorder | 96 | 95 | 85 | 88 | 83 |
| Microwave oven | 84 | 86 | 75 | 72 | 62 |
| Compact disc player | 72 | 75 | 50 | 60 | 51 |
| Tumble dryer | 71 | 66 | 52 | 56 | 44 |
| Home computer | 46 | 36 | 21 | 24 | 20 |
| Dishwasher | 33 | 32 | 22 | 12 | 11 |

*Source: General Household Survey, Office for National Statistics; Continuous Household Survey, Northern Ireland Statistics and Research Agency*

# 3.6

## Families with regular use of a car or van: by family type, 1995-96

Great Britain      Percentages

| | No car or van | One car or van | Two cars or vans | Three or more cars or vans | All |
|---|---|---|---|---|---|
| **Couples** | | | | | |
| Dependent children | 10 | 46 | 39 | 5 | 100 |
| No dependent children | 14 | 50 | 30 | 6 | 100 |
| All couples | 13 | 48 | 34 | 6 | 100 |
| **Lone parents** | | | | | |
| Dependent children | 51 | 41 | 6 | 1 | 100 |
| No dependent children | 36 | 43 | 20 | 1 | 100 |
| All lone parents | 47 | 42 | 10 | 1 | 100 |

*Source: General Household Survey, Office for National Statistics*

Although parents identified a lack of money as a key impact of having children, it is interesting to look at other indicators of living standards for families in the United Kingdom. Couples with children were more likely than those without to have most of the durable goods shown in Table 3.5 in 1995-96. One possible explanation for this might be that in some cases a particular durable good may be seen as important if children are present in the household, such as washing machines and tumble dryers.

However, when lone parents with dependent children are compared with couples with dependent children, for all the items in the table (except for black and white televisions) the proportion of couple families with each of the durables is higher than that of lone parents. Couples with dependent children were twice as likely to have a home computer, and three times as likely to have a dishwasher as lone parents. It would appear, therefore, that even though it is desirable to have certain consumer durables when children are present, the financial circumstances of lone parents do not always make this possible.

Similar distinctions emerge when looking at the levels of car ownership among family types. Nine in ten couple families with dependent children had access to a car or van which compared with only half of lone parents with dependent children (Table 3.6). Among couples with dependent children, 44 per cent had access to two or more cars or vans.

With the higher incidence of families with both parents working these days compared with the past, it might seem fair to assume

# 3.7

that there are now more 'latchkey' children, that is those who come home to empty houses, than a generation ago. However, this does not appear to be the case. A survey carried out in 1996 in Great Britain by MORI for Pillsbury UK Ltd showed that only 7 per cent of adults with children aged 6 to 18 said that their children returned home to find no-one there (Chart 3.7), although this percentage increased as the children got older. This compares with the 9 per cent who said that when they themselves were children they returned home to an empty house.

It appears to be also more common now than a generation ago for the father to be at home, with the proportion having more than doubled since the parents themselves were children. Notably, there appears to have been no reduction in the number of children coming home to their mothers.

One occasion when families have an opportunity to be together is at the evening meal time. Nine out of ten families with children eat together at least once a week, while just over four in ten eat together every day (Chart 3.8). Seven in ten families with children eat together between 5pm and 6.30pm, and Sunday is favoured slightly more than any other day.

Although Chart 3.7 implies that there is a slightly increased tendency for a parent to be at home when their children return home compared with a generation ago, nearly four in ten parents said that they now eat together as a family less often than they did when they themselves were children. This may be because, as lifestyles have become busier, snacking has increased. Three fifths

of parents claimed to buy more snack foods than ten years ago, with crisps, nuts and biscuits being especially popular, particularly among children.

Dietary patterns can vary considerably between people from different social classes. The National Diet and Nutrition Survey of children aged between one and a half and four and a half years showed clear patterns and differences in the types of foods consumed by children from different social classes. This particular age group is thought to be of key importance as there is evidence to suggest that the adoption of a healthy lifestyle in the early years of life encourages optimum growth and resistance to ill health in later life.

**Presence of family members[1] when children return home, September 1996**

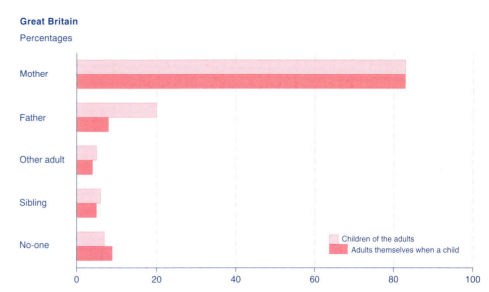

1 Parents with children aged 6 to 18 were questioned about who was present when their children returned home and when they themselves returned home as a child. Multiple responses were allowed.

**Source: MORI for Pillsbury UK Ltd**

# 3.8

**Frequency[1] with which parents and their children[2] eat their evening meal together, September 1996**

**Great Britain**

Percentages

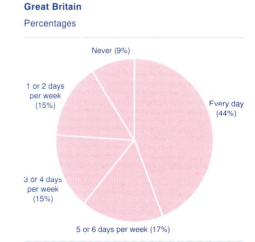

1 As reported by parents.
2 Children aged 6 to 18.

**Source: MORI for Pillsbury UK Ltd**

# 3.9

## Eating habits of young children[1]: by social class of head of household, 1992-93[2]

**Great Britain**                                                                    Grams per week

|  | Manual | Non-manual | All social classes[3] |
|---|---|---|---|
| White bread | 245 | 199 | 226 |
| Potato chips | 217 | 176 | 200 |
| Meat pies and pastries | 162 | 127 | 149 |
| Chicken and turkey dishes | 79 | 99 | 89 |
| Sugar confectionery | 125 | 103 | 115 |
| Chocolate confectionery | 109 | 91 | 101 |
| Savoury snacks | 91 | 77 | 85 |
| Sugar | 40 | 24 | 33 |
| Bananas | 228 | 239 | 234 |
| Apples and pears | 207 | 229 | 219 |
| Wholegrain and high fibre breakfast cereals | 121 | 127 | 125 |
| Other breakfast cereals | 97 | 85 | 92 |

1 Mean total quantity of food item consumed by children aged between 1½ and 4½ years as estimated for seven days.
2 July 1992 to June 1993.
3 Includes those households where social class was unknown.
**Source: National Diet and Nutrition Survey, Office for National Statistics**

# 3.10

## Cigarette smoking[1] among children: by family smoking habits and gender, 1994

**England & Wales**                                                                    Percentages

|  | Males | Females | All |
|---|---|---|---|
| **Living with both parents** |  |  |  |
| Neither parent smokes | 7 | 8 | 7 |
| Father only smokes | 9 | 10 | 10 |
| Mother only smokes | 15 | 23 | 19 |
| Both parents smoke | 10 | 21 | 15 |
| **Living with a lone parent** |  |  |  |
| Lone parent doesn't smoke | .. | .. | 13 |
| Lone parent smokes | .. | .. | 25 |
| **At least one sibling at home** |  |  |  |
| No sibling smokes | 7 | 7 | 7 |
| At least one sibling smokes | 24 | 34 | 29 |

1 Percentage aged 11 to 15 who regularly smoke at least one cigarette per week.
**Source: Smoking Among Secondary School Children, Office for National Statistics**

Young children who come from households where the head is a manual worker have a diet with less emphasis on fruit and whole grain cereals, and eat greater amounts of meat pies and pastries than children from a non-manual background (Table 3.9). In addition, children from the manual group consumed two thirds more sugar than those from the non-manual group and were also likely to have eaten more confectionery in 1992-93.

Smoking among children is a health risk of particular concern. The decision of young people to smoke can, to a great extent, be influenced by who is smoking around them, be it family or peer group. In the biennial surveys of Smoking Among Secondary School Children, pupils in secondary schools are asked (via a self-completion questionnaire) about their smoking habits. They are classified as regular smokers if they usually smoke at least one cigarette a week.

Overall, 12 per cent of 11 to 15 year old children in England and Wales were regular smokers in 1994. In this age group girls were more likely to smoke than boys, with 13 per cent of girls and 10 per cent of boys smoking regularly. Children of this age were much more likely to be smokers if other people at home smoke - their parents and, even more importantly, their brothers and sisters (Table 3.10). In 1994, children were four times as likely to smoke if at least one brother or sister smoked than if none did. The same survey also suggested that parents were perceived as being strongly opposed to their children smoking. Even in families where both parents smoked, four in five non-smoking pupils said their parents would try to stop them smoking or would persuade them not to smoke.

Smoking is not the only type of behaviour to be influenced by family members. The YLS provided information on self-reported crime by young people aged 14 to 25 in England and Wales. Young people were asked whether they had committed any offences from a list of 23, ranging from damaging or destroying the property of others to hurting someone with a knife, stick or other weapon. The person was classed as 'ever offending' if they admitted three or more minor offences or one or more serious offences from the list.

Importantly the results from this survey suggested that there is a link between admitting a crime and a range of family-related factors. For example, it was found that young people who had lived with only one parent or in a step-family when they were 14 or 15 were more likely to say they had offended than those who had lived with both natural parents. In addition, rates of self-reported offending were higher among boys than girls.

It is important to note that this does not necessarily mean that coming from a particular type of family structure causes criminal behaviour, because there are numerous other factors to be taken into account. In particular, once the quality of relationships with parents and their willingness to supervise their children were taken into account, the influence of family structure disappears. Among both boys and girls who said they had a bad relationship with their fathers when they were aged 14 or 15, the rates for admitting to having ever offended were double those of young people who claimed to have had a good relationship. Similarly, in relation to supervision, 32 per cent of boys and 14 per cent of girls who were closely supervised admitted offending compared with 53 per cent and 30 per cent respectively for those who were not (Table 3.11).

## Relationships

Many people's idea of a family is of parents with their dependent children. This, however, does not capture the full range of family relationships. Not all young adults move away from their parental home: many people in their early twenties still live with their parents. This is much more likely to occur among men than women. In 1995-96 just over half of 20 to 24 year old men in England lived with their parents, compared with just over a third of women of the same age (Table 3.12).

The National Child Development Study (NCDS) examined the living arrangements of a group of people aged 33 in 1991. The study confirmed that over 90 per cent of this group were living away from their parents or parents-in-law. Of those still living with their parents or parents-in-law, about two out of five had lived independently at some point and had then returned home.

# 3.11

**Young people ever offending[1]: by family factors[2] and gender, 1992-93[3]**

| England & Wales | | Percentages |
|---|---|---|
| | Males | Females |
| **Attachment to family** | | |
| Strong | 42 | 17 |
| Medium/weak | 70 | 33 |
| **Parental supervision** | | |
| Strong | 32 | 14 |
| Medium/weak | 53 | 30 |
| **Siblings' influence** | | |
| No siblings in trouble with police | 46 | 17 |
| Siblings in trouble with police | 68 | 55 |

1 Respondents aged 14 to 25 were categorised as an 'ever offender' if they admitted to at least three minor offences from a list of 23, or one serious offence.
2 At age 14 or 15.
3 November 1992 to January 1993.
*Source: Youth Lifestyles Survey, Home Office*

# 3.12

**Adults living with their parents: by age**

| England | | | Percentages |
|---|---|---|---|
| | 1977-78 | 1991 | 1995-96 |
| **Males** | | | |
| 20-24 | 52 | 50 | 54 |
| 25-29 | 19 | 19 | 24 |
| 30-34 | 9 | 9 | 11 |
| **Females** | | | |
| 20-24 | 31 | 32 | 36 |
| 25-29 | 9 | 9 | 11 |
| 30-34 | 3 | 5 | 5 |

*Source: National Dwelling and Household Survey and Survey of English Housing, Department of the Environment, Transport and the Regions; Labour Force Survey, Office for National Statistics*

# 3.13

## Average age at which people left the parental home[1]: by age[2], 1994-95[3]

| Great Britain | | Years |
| --- | --- | --- |
| | Males | Females |
| 16-19 | 18 | 17 |
| 20-24 | 20 | 20 |
| 25-34 | 21 | 21 |
| 35-44 | 22 | 21 |
| 45-54 | 24 | 22 |
| 55-64 | 25 | 23 |
| 65 and over | 26 | 24 |
| All aged 16 and over | 23 | 22 |

1 Excludes those who had not left the parental home.
2 Age at time of interview.
3 Main fieldwork took place between July 1994 and February 1995.

**Source: Family and Working Lives Survey, Department for Education and Employment**

As children get older and become adults they are increasingly likely to have left the parental home. The average age that they leave home has fallen over time: people who were aged 65 to 69 in 1995 reported that they were on average 25 years of age when they left their parents' home in Great Britain compared with 22 years of age for those aged 35 to 44 (Table 3.13). It should be noted that these average ages were calculated excluding those who had not left home.

Elderly people who live either alone or with people other than their children or partners are outside the scope of the nuclear family definition. In 1994-95 the General Household Survey (GHS) included a number of questions to be asked of elderly people aged 65 and over living in private households. It found that at all ages beyond 65, elderly men were more likely than elderly women to be living with a spouse (Table 3.14). In all, 61 per cent of men aged 65 and over lived with their spouse compared with only 35 per cent of women in the same age group. This reflects the differences in life expectancy between the genders as well as the likelihood that a wife will be younger than her husband. Overall, elderly women were more than three times as likely as elderly men to be living with one of their children.

# 3.14

## Living arrangements of elderly people: by gender, age and household type, 1994-95

| Great Britain | | | | | Percentages |
| --- | --- | --- | --- | --- | --- |
| | 65-69 | 70-74 | 75-79 | 80-84 | 85 and over | All aged 65 and over |
| **Males** | | | | | | |
| Lives with | | | | | | |
| Spouse/partner | 63 | 66 | 62 | 50 | 41 | 61 |
| Spouse/partner/other(s) | 13 | 9 | 9 | 3 | 5 | 9 |
| Sibling | 1 | 3 | 1 | 3 | 1 | 2 |
| Son/daughter | 2 | 2 | 3 | 3 | 2 | 2 |
| Other | 1 | 1 | 1 | 1 | 1 | 1 |
| Lives alone | 19 | 19 | 25 | 39 | 49 | 24 |
| All males | 100 | 100 | 100 | 100 | 100 | 100 |
| **Females** | | | | | | |
| Lives with | | | | | | |
| Spouse/partner | 51 | 40 | 28 | 20 | 10 | 35 |
| Spouse/partner/other(s) | 8 | 4 | 2 | 2 | 2 | 4 |
| Sibling | 1 | 2 | 3 | 4 | 3 | 2 |
| Son/daughter | 6 | 5 | 7 | 11 | 12 | 7 |
| Other | 2 | 2 | 1 | 2 | 3 | 2 |
| Live alone | 32 | 46 | 59 | 61 | 70 | 49 |
| All females | 100 | 100 | 100 | 100 | 100 | 100 |

**Source: General Household Survey, Office for National Statistics**

Even in situations where adult relatives do not live in the same household, the British Social Attitudes Survey (BSA) found that they do tend to live close to each other. The majority of people live within an hour's journey of at least one close relative. Around three in ten parents lived less than 15 minutes travelling time from their adult children in 1995 (Table 3.15). The biggest distances were those separating adult siblings with a fifth living three or more hours apart. Although high proportions of family members lived close to each other, there had been a slight decline since 1986 when 70 per cent of people lived within an hour's journey time of their mother; by 1995 this had reduced to 65 per cent.

# 3.15

Of course, living geographically close to members of the family is not a measure of whether those who do not live together keep in contact with each other. Most people do, however, see other non-resident members of their family at least once a month (Table 3.16), although this does vary according to which member of the family they see. About three quarters of parents saw a non-resident adult child at least once a month in 1995, whereas only half of adults saw an adult sibling with the same frequency. This, however, can be explained, to some extent at least, by the fact that adult siblings tend to live further apart.

The contact between a mother and her non-resident child is generally more frequent than between father and child. Almost half of adults saw their mother at least once a week in 1995, and only 3 per cent never saw her. This contrasts with 9 per cent who never saw their father. However, contact between family members is generally not as regular as between adults and their best friends: four fifths saw their best friend at least once a month and three fifths saw them at least once a week.

Compared with 1986, contact with all relatives and best friends has declined. This can be partly explained by the fact that people tended to live further away from their relatives in 1995. It is also linked to changes in the labour market, particularly the increase in the number of women working outside the home.

### Journey time[1] to non-resident adult relatives' homes, 1995

**Great Britain**                                                                                                    Percentages

|  | Less than 15 minutes | 15 minutes to 1 hour | 1 to 3 hours | 3 or more hours | Not answered | All |
|---|---|---|---|---|---|---|
| Mother | 31 | 34 | 17 | 16 | 2 | 100 |
| Father | 28 | 30 | 17 | 18 | 7 | 100 |
| Adult sibling | 23 | 37 | 19 | 20 | 1 | 100 |
| Adult child | 30 | 37 | 14 | 10 | 9 | 100 |
| Other relative | 30 | 36 | 17 | 15 | 2 | 100 |

1 By people aged 18 and over. Time taken, door to door, to get to relatives' homes by whatever form of transport. Those without the relative in question or living with the relative were excluded.

**Source: British Social Attitudes Survey, Social & Community Planning Research**

# 3.16

### Frequency[1] of seeing non-resident adult relatives, 1995

**Great Britain**                                                                                                    Percentages

|  | Daily | Less than daily but at least once a week | Less than once a week but at least once a month | Less often | Never | Not answered | All |
|---|---|---|---|---|---|---|---|
| Mother | 8 | 40 | 21 | 27 | 3 | 1 | 100 |
| Father | 6 | 33 | 20 | 29 | 9 | 3 | 100 |
| Adult sibling | 4 | 25 | 21 | 45 | 4 | 1 | 100 |
| Adult child | 10 | 48 | 16 | 18 | 1 | 7 | 100 |
| Other relative | 3 | 31 | 26 | 37 | 1 | 2 | 100 |

1 By people aged 18 and over. Those without the relative in question or living with the relative were excluded.

**Source: British Social Attitudes Survey, Social & Community Planning Research**

# 3.17

**Regular contact between people in full-time employment and their mothers[1]: by gender, 1986 and 1995**

| Great Britain | | Percentages |
|---|---|---|
| | 1986 | 1995 |
| Males | *49* | *46* |
| Females | *64* | *45* |

*1 Percentage of people aged 18 and over, working 30 or more hours per week, who see their non-resident mother at least once a week. Those without a living mother were excluded.*

**Source: British Social Attitudes Survey, Social & Community Planning Research**

# 3.18

**Frequency of contact between non-resident fathers and their children[1], 1995-96[2]**

**Great Britain**

Percentages

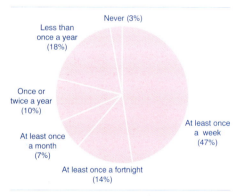

Never (3%)
Less than once a year (18%)
Once or twice a year (10%)
At least once a month (7%)
At least once a fortnight (14%)
At least once a week (47%)

*1 Dependent children who normally live with their mother in another household. Excludes fathers whose children are away at boarding school or in care, residential home or hostel.*
*2 April 1995 to April 1996.*

**Source: Social Policy Research Unit, University of York**

Table 3.17 demonstrates this point in more detail. Focusing on the contact between people in full-time employment and their non-resident mothers, it shows that the proportion of men in full-time work who saw their mother at least once a week changed little between 1986 and 1995. The decline among women in full-time work who saw their mothers this often has, in contrast, been particularly noticeable, dropping by nearly a third from 64 per cent to 45 per cent. On the one hand this has narrowed the gap between men and women while, on the other, it would suggest some significant change in the nature of full-time work in which women are engaged that has not been experienced in the same way by men. It might, for example, suggest greater parity between the pressures that men and women are now put under in the workplace, or alternatively an increase in the time commitment required from work. However, it is not just contact with relatives which has decreased. It appears that people are generally less likely to visit, or be visited by, anyone, as demonstrated by the fall in regularity with which people see their best friends.

In terms of the amount of contact, the relationship between a mother and her children is generally stronger than between a father and his children. The launch of the *Child Support Act 1991* has focused attention on non-resident fathers. Until recently very little was actually known about the characteristics of absent fathers. A study by the Social Policy Research Unit at the University of York showed that nine tenths of absent fathers had at some time been married to, or cohabited with, the mother of their child. Just over half lived apart from only one child, while one in nine lived apart from three or more children. The majority of fathers had not gone on to form new families: nearly 60 per cent were living without a partner.

Most absent fathers keep in contact with their children. Almost half saw their children at least once a week (Chart 3.18), and only 3 per cent never saw their child. Just over half (55 per cent) felt they did not have enough control over when they saw their children and 44 per cent thought they did not see their children often enough. The study also found that three fifths of fathers were making maintenance payments, with the weekly average being £26 per child in 1995-96, or £16 per child if the father was unemployed. Overall, the study concluded that the great majority of absent fathers were attempting, albeit with some difficulty, to maintain relationships with their children.

The level of contact between family members, when viewed in isolation, does not say anything about the quality of the contact that takes place, or the closeness of the family unit. One way of considering these issues is to look at the types of advice and support that the family provides in times of difficulty. When faced with a variety of potential problems, people will turn to

# 3.19

different sources for help. If the problem is a household job the first person who people turn to for help tends to be a spouse or partner (Table 3.19). Spouses and partners also play an important role where the problem is depression. The failure to turn to a partner or spouse in the case of marital difficulties is perhaps unsurprising. However, around one in twelve people said they would not turn to anyone when they were in this situation, and only one in fifty said that they would use marital counselling. There were also gender differences: for example, 11 per cent of men would not seek anyone's support, compared with only 5 per cent of women.

To whom someone decides to turn for help is of course influenced by who is available. For example, in the case of depression, two thirds of people who were married or cohabiting said that they would turn to their partner, whereas those who were either separated, divorced or single said that they were most likely to turn to friends. In contrast, widows or widowers were most likely to seek the support of their children most often.

The British Social Attitudes Survey also asked people about sums of money over £100 that they had loaned or given as a gift to relatives or others, and the sources of money over the same value which they themselves had received as loans or gifts. Three in ten people had received money as a loan or gift in the past five years. Table

**First person adults[1] would turn to for help: by type of problem, 1995**

| Great Britain | | | | | Percentages |
|---|---|---|---|---|---|
| | Household job | Help while ill | Borrowing money | Marital problems | Depression |
| Spouse/partner | 58 | 61 | 21 | 9 | 47 |
| Child | 13 | 11 | 6 | 17 | 7 |
| Parent | 8 | 13 | 20 | 15 | 8 |
| Sibling | 4 | 3 | 4 | 12 | 6 |
| Friend | 7 | 5 | 2 | 27 | 21 |
| No-one | 1 | 1 | 7 | 8 | 3 |
| Bank | . | . | 32 | . | . |
| Other[2] | 8 | 5 | 5 | 10 | 7 |
| Not answered | 1 | 1 | 2 | 3 | 2 |
| All | 100 | 100 | 100 | 100 | 100 |

1 People aged 18 and over.
2 Includes other relatives, work colleagues, home and paid help, church, clergy or priest, family doctor, psychologist, marriage guidance counsellor and health visitor.
*Source: British Social Attitudes Survey, Social & Community Planning Research*

# 3.20

3.20 gives a detailed breakdown of the sources of money received and demonstrates that a parent or parent-in-law was the most common source of loans or gifts. Perhaps a little surprisingly a friend was a more common source of a loan or gift than a spouse or partner. This, however, might be partly due to the fact that in many relationships financial resources may be shared.

For the last 40 years it has been government policy that sick and disabled people should be cared for in the community wherever possible. As well as the health and welfare services that make this possible, a large role is also played by family and friends who provide support informally.

**Sources of money received as a loan or gift[1]: by gender, 1995**

| Great Britain | | Percentages |
|---|---|---|
| | Males | Females |
| Spouse/partner | 6 | 3 |
| Parent/parent-in-law | 60 | 58 |
| Other family member | 16 | 22 |
| Friend | 7 | 6 |
| Other[2] | 5 | 5 |
| Not answered | 6 | 5 |
| All | 100 | 100 |

1 People aged 18 and over were asked: 'In the past five years have you personally received a loan or gift of £100 or more from an adult relative, friend, neighbour or colleague to help with some emergency or problem?'.
2 Includes 'mother and father', 'daughter and son', 'sister and brother', 'aunt and uncle'.
*Source: British Social Attitudes Survey, Social & Community Planning Research*

# 3.21

### Adults[1] who care for sick, elderly or disabled relatives: by gender, 1990-91

| Great Britain | | | Percentages |
|---|---|---|---|
| | Males | Females | All |
| **Caring for** | | | |
| Spouse | 1.6 | 1.6 | 1.6 |
| Child under 16 | 0.3 | 0.4 | 0.4 |
| Child aged 16 and over | 0.5 | 0.6 | 0.6 |
| Parent | 4.9 | 7.4 | 6.3 |
| Parent-in-law | 3.1 | 2.3 | 2.7 |
| Other relative | 3.1 | 3.9 | 3.5 |

1 People aged 16 and over.

**Source: General Household Survey, Office for National Statistics**

# 3.22

### Family events[1] regarded as important, 1994-95

**Great Britain**

Percentages

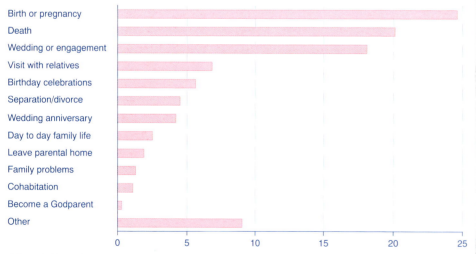

1 Events in the previous year that people aged 16 and over regarded as important. Up to four events could be reported.

**Source: British Household Panel Survey, ESRC Research Centre on Micro-social Change**

Periodically, the General Household Survey (GHS) includes questions on carers. The latest available information relates to 1990-91, when 15 per cent of people aged 16 and over were either looking after someone sick, elderly or disabled in their own household, or providing regular help and support to someone outside their household. The survey found that 11 per cent of carers spent 50 hours or more caring per week. Table 3.21 shows the percentage of adults who were caring for immediate family or other relatives in 1990-91. The most likely recipients of this care were parents. While, at 7 per cent, more women than men were caring for a parent, there were nevertheless 5 per cent of men looking after these relatives. The likelihood of caring for relatives other than parents was very similar for men and women.

Fifty-seven per cent of the carers were looking after someone who was aged 75 or over and 71 per cent were looking after a female dependent. The type of help being provided varied in its nature, from personal care such as washing and dressing, to other practical support such as shopping, housework and gardening. It is important to bear in mind that keeping the dependent company is also an important part of the informal carer's role. Questions about carers were included again in the 1995-96 GHS. The results of these will be published in a report in Summer 1997.

As well as the interdependencies and support networks that exist within families, family events also have an impact on the way individuals relate to each other. In 1994-95, the British Household Panel Survey asked people about important events that had happened to themselves or their families during the course of the year. Those taking part in the survey were able to mention up to four events, and 44 per cent of all cases where specific events were mentioned related to the family. Both males and females mentioned family events more than other types of event such as employment, leisure and health. Family events that were mentioned as important covered a broad range of issues, but generally they tended to reflect times of change in family life.

Analysis of only the family events mentioned showed that just under one in four were births, and one in five deaths, with weddings or engagements being the third most often mentioned (Chart 3.22). Together, these three accounted for 63 per cent of all mentions of family events. The 'other' category included events such as adoptions. There were differences in mentions of family events by age and gender. For example, younger men aged 16 to 24 were more likely to mention employment events than family ones. For women in the same age group, on the other hand, mentions of family events were the most frequent.

Christmas is traditionally the time of year particularly associated with family celebration. When Gallup questioned people in December 1996 about whether or not they would take part in a family gathering at Christmas, the large majority expected that they would (Chart 3.23). Half of all people questioned said that they believed Christmas was mainly an occasion for having a pleasant time with family and friends. This compares with 17 per cent of people who said that they believed it was mainly a religious occasion, and 29 per cent who thought that both were important.

Although Christmas is seen as a time for being with the family, it is not without its problems. One in ten people said that they had experienced a family row over the previous festive season, although the majority of these proved not to be particularly serious and from which everybody recovered fairly quickly.

In December 1994 the Department of Health set up a parenting initiative. As well as providing support for parenting programmes, the initiative also included a study to establish how parents sought help in everyday situations where they had problems in bringing up their children. The most common problems for which parents had ever sought outside help were related to health (Chart 3.24). This covered a range of complaints, from disability or handicap to asthma and bed-wetting. Abuse and attack accounted for 13 per cent of the problems reported by parents for which they had sought outside help. This included physical

and sexual abuse as well as bullying or teasing outside the school environment. Family problems were particularly diverse, touching on issues such as custody of children, children taken into care and difficulties with adopted, foster or step-children. Family problems were particularly prevalent for working lone parents, where 28 per cent of the problems reported were of this type.

It is interesting that housing tenure showed links with reports of particular types of problems. For example, the highest incidence of parents seeking outside help for behavioural and crime-related problems came from those parents who rented from local authorities or housing associations. Owner-occupiers with a mortgage, in contrast, were around twice as likely as those who were renting to report seeking

### Expectations of taking part in a family gathering at Christmas[1], December 1996

**Great Britain**
Percentages

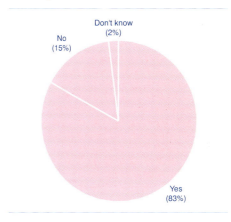

1 Adults aged 18 and over were asked: 'Will you be taking part in a family gathering this Christmas or not?'.
**Source: Gallup**

# 3.24

### Parenting[1] problems for which outside help[2] had ever been sought, January to April 1995

**Great Britain**
Percentages

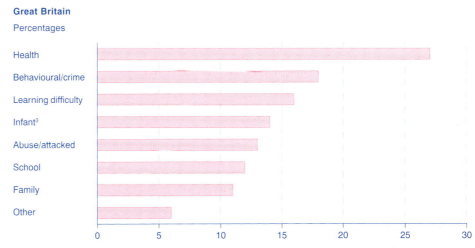

1 Those with a child (or whose partner had a child) aged under 18 living with them or elsewhere, or those who were a guardian with a child aged under 16 in the household.
2 Includes help from a relative or friend as well as other sources like GPs, teachers, ministers, the police or social services.
3 Problems experienced by children under one year, such as colic.
**Source: Omnibus Survey, Office for National Statistics**

# 3.25

## Children on child protection registers: by gender and category, 1995[1]

| England, Wales & Northern Ireland | | Percentages |
|---|---|---|
| | Males | Females |
| Physical injury only | 32 | 26 |
| Neglect only | 27 | 24 |
| Sexual abuse only | 16 | 26 |
| Emotional abuse only | 14 | 13 |
| Multiple categories | 8 | 9 |
| Other[2] | 3 | 3 |
| All children (=100%) | | |
| (thousands) | 19.2 | 18.8 |

1 At 31 March.
2 Includes 'grave concern' in Northern Ireland.
*Source: Department of Health; Welsh Office; Department of Health and Social Services, Northern Ireland*

# 3.26

## ChildLine enquiries[1]: by type of problem, 1986-87[2] and 1995-96

| United Kingdom | | Percentages |
|---|---|---|
| | 1986-87[2] | 1995-96 |
| Family relationship | 20 | 15 |
| Bullying | 3 | 11 |
| Physical abuse | 18 | 10 |
| Sexual abuse | 27 | 9 |
| Problem with friends | 4 | 9 |
| Pregnancy | 6 | 8 |
| Runaway | 2 | 3 |
| School | 2 | 2 |
| Substance abuse | 2 | 2 |
| Health | 1 | 2 |
| Risk of abuse | 3 | 1 |
| Self abuse | 1 | 1 |
| Bereavement | - | 1 |
| Other problems | 11 | 27 |
| All enquiries (=100%) | | |
| (thousands) | 23.5 | 89.8 |

1 First time callers and letter writers only.
2 Data relate to year to 31 October 1987, the first year of ChildLine.
*Source: ChildLine*

help for dyslexia, speech or learning disabilities. However, this is likely to reflect socio-economic and financial circumstances, for example, being able to afford particular types of outside help, such as extra tuition. Since health problems were the most commonly reported, it is unsurprising to find that in 26 per cent of all problems the first person approached for help was a doctor. A nurse, midwife or health visitor was the first person approached in 18 per cent of cases. In 21 per cent of cases, the first person approached was a teacher.

In addition to parents seeking help for particular problems, an important function of social services is to help children who are considered to be at risk. Each social services department holds a register that lists children in the area who are considered to be at risk of abuse. Registration takes place following a case conference and once on the register an inter-agency agreement is drawn up to protect the child. It is important to note that the registers are not records of child abuse. Some children on the register will not actually have been subject to abuse, and others who have been abused will not have been placed on the register if there is no need for a protection plan.

Table 3.25 shows that in March 1995, 38 thousand children in England, Wales and Northern Ireland were on the child protection register. The most common reason for boys being on the register was the risk of physical injury alone, with a third of boys registered considered at risk from this type of abuse. For girls there was no risk category that was significantly more widespread than the others, with risk of physical injury, neglect and sexual abuse, each accounting for approximately a quarter of all registrations.

Children may be considered to be at risk from more than one type of abuse, and around one in twelve children on the register fell into this category.

As well as abuse within the family, young people can be beset by many of the same problems experienced by adults, including alcohol and drug abuse, as well as problems more specific to children such as bullying and problems at school. Launched in 1986, ChildLine provides a 24-hour confidential counselling service that children in the United Kingdom with any form of problem can contact for advice, comfort and protection.

In 1995-96 ChildLine counselled 90 thousand children, nearly four times as many as in the first year in 1986-87 (Table 3.26). Although the overall proportion of contacts about physical abuse fell from about 18 per cent in the first year to 10 per cent in 1995-96, the number of calls more than doubled over the period, from 4.2 thousand to 8.9 thousand. The number of calls about bullying increased at a far greater rate than calls for any other reason during this period, partly due to a high profile campaign about this issue. About a quarter of the calls in 1995-96 fell into the 'other' category, which includes adoption, domestic violence, suicide and concern for others. The ratio of girls to boys calling was around four to one.

While there has been a shift in the way families are organised in terms of living arrangements and the regularity with which their members see each other, these could be seen more as a symptom of broader socio-economic changes, such as those in the labour market, and less to do with negative attitudes towards the concept of the family. Families can continue to play an important role in people's lives. Table 3.27 illustrates this notion, showing that 70 per cent of people in Great Britain in 1995 believed that contact should be maintained with close family members even if they have little in common. Even with regard to the extended family such as aunts, uncles and cousins, just over half of people agreed with staying in touch.

Perhaps the most solid evidence that family bonds remain strong is that only 13 per cent of people said they would rather spend time with friends than with their family, and just 7 per cent said that their friends were more important than members of their family. So, despite the problems that can be experienced by family members, individually or as a whole, the family as an institution is far from being in decline.

### Attitudes[1] towards the family, 1995

| Great Britain | | | | | Percentages |
|---|---|---|---|---|---|
| | Strongly agree/ agree | Neither agree nor disagree | Disagree/ strongly disagree | Can't choose/ not answered | All |
| People should keep in touch with close family members even if they don't have much in common | 70 | 18 | 10 | 3 | 100 |
| People should keep in touch with relatives like aunts, uncles and cousins even if they don't have much in common | 55 | 31 | 12 | 3 | 100 |
| People should always turn to their family before asking the state for help | 48 | 19 | 29 | 4 | 100 |
| I try to stay in touch with all my relatives, not just my close family | 46 | 22 | 27 | 5 | 100 |
| I'd rather spend time with my friends than with my family | 13 | 23 | 59 | 5 | 100 |
| Once children have left home, they should no longer expect help from their parents | 12 | 13 | 72 | 3 | 100 |
| On the whole, my friends are more important to me than members of my family | 7 | 12 | 76 | 4 | 100 |

1 People aged 18 and over were asked how much they agreed or disagreed with each statement, on a 5-point scale ranging from 'strongly agree' to 'strongly disagree'.

**Source: British Social Attitudes Survey, Social & Community Planning Research**

# References and further reading

### General

*Annual Abstract of Statistics*, The Stationery Office

*A Statistical Portrait of Youth Exclusion. A Siena Group Monitoring Report*, ISTAT

*British Social Attitudes*, Dartmouth Publishing

*Changing Households: The British Household Panel Survey*, ESRC Research Centre on Micro-social Change

*Families in Britain, Family Report 3*, Family Policy Studies Centre

*Family Change and Future Policy*, Family Policy Studies Centre

*Living in Britain*, The Stationery Office

*Monthly Digest of Statistics*, The Stationery Office

*Population Trends*, The Stationery Office

*Regional Trends*, The Stationery Office

*Sexual Behaviour in Britain, The National Survey of Sexual Attitudes and Lifestyles*, Penguin Books

*Social Focus on Children*, The Stationery Office

*Social Focus on Ethnic Minorities*, The Stationery Office

*Social Focus on Women*, The Stationery Office

*Social Trends*, The Stationery Office

*The Family*, David Willetts, WH Smith Contemporary Papers

### Family dynamics

*Birth Statistics - England and Wales 1995, Series FM1*, The Stationery Office

*Children looked after by Local Authorities*, Department of Health

*Key Population and Vital Statistics, Series VS/PP1*, The Stationery Office

*Marriage and Divorce statistics - England and Wales 1994, Series FM2*, The Stationery Office

*Marriage and the Family Law Act 1996*, Lord Chancellor's Department

*National Family Mediation's Guidance to Separation and Divorce*, T Fisher, Vermillion

*Stability and Instability in Children's Family Lives: Longitudinal Evidence from Two British Sources*, City University

*Who's at Home at 33?, National Child Development Study Working Paper 42*, City University

### Family living standards

*Economic Trends*, The Stationery Office

*English House Condition Survey*, The Stationery Office

*Family Resources Survey*, The Stationery Office

*Family Spending*, The Stationery Office

*Households Below Average Income, A Statistical Analysis*, The Stationery Office

*Housing Finance*, Council of Mortgage Lenders

*Housing in England*, The Stationery Office

*Labour Force Survey Historical Supplement*, Office for National Statistics

*Labour Force Survey Quarterly Bulletin*, Office for National Statistics

*Labour Market Trends (incorporating Employment Gazette)*, The Stationery Office

*More Work in Fewer Households?*, P Gregg and J Wadsworth, London School of Economics

*Social Security Departmental Report*, The Stationery Office

*Social Security Statistics*, The Stationery Office

**Family life**

*ChildLine Annual Report*, ChildLine

*General Household Survey: Carers in 1990*, The Stationery Office

*Informal Carers*, The Stationery Office

*National Diet and Nutrition Survey, Volume 1: Report of the Diet and Nutrition Survey*, The
  Stationery Office

*Non-resident Fathers in Britain*, University of York

*Parenting Problems: A National Study of Parents and Parenting Problems*, Family Policy
  Studies Centre

*Smoking Among Secondary School Children in 1994*, The Stationery Office

*Value of a Mum Survey*, Research Services Ltd

*Young People and Crime, Research Study 145*, Home Office Research and Planning Unit

# Contact points

General information about *Social Focus on Families* can be obtained from the editorial team at the Office for National Statistics; tel 0171 533 5782. Other contacts are given below:

**Biss Lancaster**
    Family Eating Survey      0171 497 3001

**ChildLine**      0171 239 1093

**City University**
    Social Statistics Research Unit      0171 477 8484

**Department for Education and Employment**
    Family and Working Lives Survey      0171 273 4879

**Department of Economic Development, Northern Ireland**
    Income      01232 529383
    Labour market      01232 529550

**Department of Health**      0171 972 5553
    Foster placements      0171 972 5573

**Department of Health and Social Services, Northern Ireland**      01232 522961

**Department of National Heritage**      0171 211 2110

**Department of Social Security**
    Benefits      0191 225 5674
    Family Resources Survey      0171 962 8092
    Households Below Average Income      0171 962 8232

**Department of the Environment, Transport and the Regions**      0171 890 3301

**Department of the Environment, Northern Ireland**      01232 540808

**ESRC Research Centre for Analysis of Social Exclusion,
London School of Economics**      0171 955 6679

**ESRC Research Centre for Micro-social Change**      01206 872957

**Family Policy Studies Centre**      0171 486 8211

**Gallup**      0181 336 6400

**Home Office**
    Youth Lifestyles Survey      0171 273 3960

**Legal and General Group plc**                            01737 370370

**Ministry of Agriculture, Fisheries and Food**            0171 270 8547

**Northern Ireland Statistics and Research Agency**

    Continuous Household Survey               01232 252521

**Office for National Statistics**

    Children smoking                          0171 533 5331

    Effects of taxes and benefits            0171 533 5770

    Families and children                    0171 533 5121

    Family Expenditure Survey                0171 533 5754

    Fertility statistics                     0171 533 5119

    General Household Survey                  0171 533 5444

    Labour market enquiry line               0171 533 6176

    Longitudinal Study                       0171 533 5185

    Omnibus Survey                           0171 533 5310

    Time Use Survey                          0171 533 5785

**Social & Community Planning Research**           0171 250 1866 ext 369

**University of York**

    Institute for Research in the Social Sciences     01904 433480

**Welsh Office**                                           01222 825080

# Appendix: data sources

## Major surveys used in *Social Focus on Families*

| | Frequency | Sampling Frame | Type of respondent | Country | Set sample size (most recent survey included in *Social Focus*) | Response rate (percentages) |
|---|---|---|---|---|---|---|
| British Household Panel Survey | Annual | Postal addresses | All adults in household | GB | 9,249 adults | 70[1] |
| British Social Attitudes Survey | Annual | Postcode Address File | Adult in household | GB | 5,251 addresses | 69 |
| Census of Population | Decennial | Detailed local | Household head | UK | Full count | 98 |
| Continuous Household Survey | Continuous | Ratings Valuation List | All adults in household | NI | 4,500 addresses | 78 |
| Family and Working Lives Survey | One-off | Postcode Address File | Adult aged 16-69 and any partner | GB | 16,987 households[2] | 54 |
| Family Expenditure Survey | Continuous | Postcode Address File | Household in GB, Rating List in NI | UK | 10,150 addresses[2] | 66[3] |
| Family Resources Survey | Continuous | Postcode Address File | All adults in household | GB | 26,435 households | 70 |
| General Household Survey | Continuous | Postcode Address File | All adults in household | GB | 11,914 households | 80 |
| Labour Force Survey | Continuous | Postcode Address File | All adults in household[4] | UK | 60,321 households[5] | 80[5] |
| Omnibus Survey | Continuous | Postcode Address File | One adult per household | GB | 3,000 addresses[6] | 71[6] |
| Survey of English Housing | Continuous | Postcode Address File | Household | E | 25,000 addresses | 80 |
| Youth Lifestyles Survey | One-off | Postcode Address File | Young people aged 14 to 25 | E&W | 3,690 households[7] | 69 |

1 Wave on wave response rate at wave 5.
2 Basic sample only.
3 Response rate refers to Great Britain.
4 Includes some proxy information.
5 Response rate to first wave interviews quoted. Response rate to second and fifth wave interviews 95 per cent of these previously accepting.
6 The Omnibus Survey changes from month to month. The sample size and response rate are for May 1996.
7 Includes a booster sample of ethnic minority young people.

# Index

# Index

**H**
Households
  adults in, by gender, age and family
    type 12
  adults living with parents 57
  by gender and family type 10
  number of 10
  people in 10
Household tasks
  performed by young people 53
  time spent on 52
Housing
  dissatisfaction with 47
  homelessness 48, 49
  mortgage and rent arrears 48, 49
  overcrowding 46
  problems with neighbours 47
  standards 46
  tenure
      following divorce 48
      link with parenting
        problems 63
      of families 44
  type of dwelling 45
  under-occupation 46
  with central heating 46

**I**
Income
  children in families below half mean
    income 37
  equivalised income 35
  net weekly spending power 40
  sources, by family type 36
Income distribution
  adults moving within 37
  dependent children in families
    within 37
  families within 36

**L**
Loans
  from family 61
Lone parents
  benefit receipt 38
  by age 26
  by gender 25, 26
  by marital status 25
  changes experienced by 26
  housing 45

**M**
Marriage
  age combinations 17
  attitudes towards 14
  average age at 16
  breakdown 13
  by birth cohort 17
  by gender 17
  by previous marital status 16
  pre-marital cohabitation 15
  rates 16
  remarriage of women 20
  status of lone parents 25
  women separated within five
    years of 18
Meals
  eating together as a family 55
Money
  sources of loans or gifts 61

**P**
Parenthood
  attitudes towards 14
  impact on social contacts 53
  impact on working arrangements 30
Parenting problems 63
Pocket money 43

**R**
Relatives
  adults living with parents 57
  cared for 62
  contact with mothers 60
  frequency of visiting 59
  journey times to non-resident
    relatives 59
Remarriages 16

**S**
Savings
  accounts held 41
  by family type 40, 41
Separation
  within five years of marriage 18
Smoking
  habits of children 56, 57
Social class
  eating habits of children 56
  median interval between marriage
    and first birth 22
  of families 11
Stepfamilies 27

**T**
Time use 52

**W**
Women
  pre-marital cohabitation 15
  remarriage 20
  returning to work following birth of
    child 31, 32
  separation within five years of
    marriage 18
Working hours
  average per week 34, 35
  impact on family life 34